PREACHING PAUL

Preaching
Paul

Brad R. Braxton

Abingdon Press
Nashville

PREACHING PAUL

This book is printed on acid-free paper.

Library of Congress Cataloging-in-Publication Data

Braxton, Brad Ronnell.
    Preaching Paul/Brad R. Braxton.
      p. cm.
    Includes bibliographical references and index.
    ISBN 0-687-02144-8 (pbk. : alk. paper)
    1. Bible. N.T. Epistles of Paul—Homiletical use.   2. Preaching—Biblical teaching.
    I. Title.

    BS2650.55.B73 2004
    227'.06—dc22

2004016937

04 05 06 07 08 09 10 11 12 13—10 9 8 7 6 5 4 3 2 1

MANUFACTURED IN THE UNITED STATES OF AMERICA

To Gary Anderson, Harry Gamble, and Judith Kovacs
my undergraduate biblical studies professors

Contents

ACKNOWLEDGMENTS

During the 2000 meeting of the Academy of Homiletics, Robert Ratcliff, Senior Editor at Abingdon Press, invited me to write this book. His invitation allowed me to combine two of my scholarly passions in one book: homiletics and New Testament studies. Also, his suggestions greatly improved the clarity and accessibility of the book.

The lectures upon which this book was founded were first delivered at the 2001 Furman Pastors School in Greenville, South Carolina. I am indebted to Jim Pitts and his colleagues for their generous hospitality. The clergy and laypersons in attendance warmly received the lectures. Their enthusiastic response convinced me that I was moving in the right direction.

Subsequently, I lectured on this material at the Indianapolis Center for Congregations; Memphis Theological Seminary; Wake Forest University; Virginia University of Lynchburg; Wilshire Baptist Church in Dallas, Texas; McCormick Theological Seminary; and Barton College. On every occasion and at every place, those in attendance met me with kind spirits and incisive minds.

A vast network of family, friends, and colleagues supplied their energy, encouragement, and expertise to this project. I might write books, but my wife Lazetta reads me like a book. With pinpoint accuracy, she discerns my emotions, corrects my imbalances, and motivates me to trust my intuitions. During the book's composition, she halted her professional career to pursue a graduate degree in business. On many occasions, we burned the midnight oil together. We were engaged in different intellectual projects but always united in spirit. Also, our cocker spaniel,

Alaké, provided additional companionship as I wrote. Playing with an appreciative puppy is a great cure for writer's block.

My parents, the Reverend James and Mrs. Louise Braxton, have touched my life in such beautiful ways, leaving their godly fingerprints all over my soul. As long as my life shall last, I will bless their names.

My sister Chanda Braxton Hill and "big brother" Nigel Alston read the manuscript and constantly challenged me to avoid academic jargon. Nigel and Gail O'Day, of Emory University, graciously agreed to write critiques of two of the sermons in the book. Shawn Adams, of Saint Paul's Episcopal Church in Winston-Salem, and Emerson Powery, of Lee University, tightened my prose and clarified my arguments.

Steven Fine, of the University of Cincinnati, offered invaluable feedback on my thinking about Paul's Pharisaic heritage. The bibliographic recommendations of the following professors greatly facilitated the book's annotated bibliography: Jouette Bassler of Southern Methodist University, Beverly Roberts Gaventa of Princeton Theological Seminary, Judith Gundry-Volf of Yale University, Carl Holladay of Emory University, and Carolyn Osiek of the Catholic Theological Union. Peter Henry of Stanford University is an unwavering source of spiritual and intellectual inspiration.

During the publication process, I assumed a professorship at Vanderbilt Divinity School. Chancellor Gordon Gee, Dean James Hudnut-Beumler, and my colleagues have eagerly welcomed me to Vanderbilt. While on the faculty of Wake Forest University Divinity School, I composed this book. I am grateful for the support of President Thomas K. Hearn Jr. and Dean Bill J. Leonard of Wake Forest University. Sherry Magill and Edward King Jr., of the Jessie Ball duPont Fund, generously endowed my professorship at Wake Forest. Also, my Wake Forest colleagues Linda McKinnish Bridges, Jill Crainshaw, Neal Walls, and Sam F. Weber, O.S.B. offered perceptive critiques that refined the book. In the fall of 2003, the students in my Preaching from the Old Testament course at Wake Forest Divinity School sharpened my reflections on the relationship between preaching and scripture.

At various stages of the book's composition I was blessed to work with extremely bright and motivated graduate research assistants. Were it not for Heather Cronk, Cheryl Garrison, Noel Schoonmaker, and Amy Steele, *Preaching Paul* would still be an idea in my mind. Their meticulous research and editing vastly improved every page of the book.

In Pauline fashion, I bid grace and peace to the members of the Douglas Memorial Community Church in Baltimore, Maryland— the people I was privileged to shepherd for five years. Douglas Church provided a challenging, invigorating, and supportive context to practice the craft of preaching. I also thank the many pastors and congregants who have allowed me to stand in their pulpits. Pulpit space and time are gifts that I never take for granted.

I dedicate this book to three biblical scholars who are very responsible for my presence in the theological academy: professors Gary Anderson, Harry Gamble, and Judith Kovacs. I began my academic study of the Bible as an undergraduate at the University of Virginia. Under the tutelage of these gifted scholars and teachers I learned that deep thinking about the Bible and deep piety inspired by the Bible could complement each other. More than a decade has passed since I studied with them. But their passion for biblical studies kindled an unquenchable flame in me. In some small way I hope this book conveys my enduring gratitude for their instruction and influence.

Finally, I pray that this book, in spite of its shortcomings, will please and glorify God.

Introduction

Truth in Advertising: Is This Book for You?

Preachers tell the truth. Or at least we are supposed to. Since I am a preacher, and this book's main subject is preaching, let me do a little "truth-telling" from the very beginning. This book is not for everyone. You might want to keep reading this book only if you fit one or more of the following profiles:

- You aspire to some form of lay or ordained Christian ministry or are in training for that ministry, and you are trying to figure out what it means to preach.

- You have just begun a lay or ordained Christian ministry, and you want to improve the substance and refine the style of your preaching.

- You are an experienced preacher with honed pulpit skills who wants to add new perspectives to your reflection on and practice of preaching.

- You are an experienced preacher who desperately needs fresh winds of inspiration to fill your flagging sails.

- You are *not* a preacher (and *never* want to be one). Yet you occasionally or regularly hear sermons and want to think more critically about the task of preaching.

- You are a passionate fan or severe critic of the early Christian apostle Paul and his writings, and you are in search of arguments for or against your position.

- You know little or nothing about the early Christian apostle Paul, and you want to know why so many people admire, detest, or study him.

- You are a student of preaching or of biblical studies, and you want to consider the relationship between preaching and the Bible. In particular, you are interested to know how preaching influenced Paul's Letters and how those letters might be vehicles for a compelling proclamation of the gospel in the twenty-first century.

If any (or many) of these criteria apply to you, keep reading. This book might be worth your time and effort.

Since This Book Is for You . . .

For those readers still with me, allow me to present the agenda of the book. This is a book about preaching. This is a book about Paul. This is a book about preaching Paul. Each of these statements deserves fuller explanation.

A Book About Preaching: A Pragmatic Approach

This book will be a guide for persons who want to explore the homiletical, biblical, and theological issues surrounding preaching in general and preaching from texts written by the apostle Paul in particular. Primarily, this book is designed to aid more faithful practice—whether that practice is improved preparation and presentation of sermons or more disciplined hearing and living of sermons. Thus, in the first chapter, I present three defining characteristics of responsible Christian proclamation. Admittedly, this characterization is risky. Given the incredible influence that congregational and cultural dynamics play on perceptions of preaching and its effectiveness, there is no one encompassing understanding of preaching that holds in all times and places.

Some readers might find my description of preaching appealing and want to adopt my understanding. Other readers might find it problematic in parts or in its entirety. Nevertheless, my characterization might prove beneficial even to its detractors.

Often in the process of arguing against a position persons argue more clearly for the position they hold. Thus a strong critique of my perception of preaching might facilitate among those who read this book a more definitive articulation of the advantages and disadvantages of their perceptions of preaching. Undoubtedly my description of preaching aims to persuade readers. I myself would not read a book about preaching—the art of faithful persuasion—if it did not try to persuade me about something. A book about preaching ought to do a little preaching. Even if my perception of preaching is less than persuasive to some, its bold presentation might still benefit the unpersuaded.

Let me affirm that preaching is a *liturgical* deed. The Greek word from which we derive "liturgical," *leitourgia*, means worship. Thus, preaching is a central component of communal worship. By worship I mean the reverent and expectant gathering of God's people around the story and practices of Christianity whereby people glorify God and God transforms people.[1]

As a liturgical *deed*, preaching is an intentional presentation of human words and gestures designed to mediate an encounter with God. At its noblest, preaching is more than a human event. It can become the occasion for a divine event—a gracious revelation of God.[2] Preaching is a human practice latent with divine possibilities.

As an aid to persons engaged in important religious practices, this book seeks to be pragmatic in its orientation. The Greek word for "deed" or "event" is *pragma*, which gives us our English word *pragmatic*. Thus to be pragmatic is to be profoundly concerned with deeds, events, and practices.[3] Some persons who read this book are regularly involved in religious practices. They might be on their way to a pulpit soon to preach a sermon or to a pew to hear a sermon.

Of course, a commitment to the pragmatic is not a denial of critical reflection. By *practicing* critical solid thinking, one quickly perceives the fallacy of establishing "action" and "reflection" as mutually exclusive. Reflection itself is a practice.[4] Anyone doubting whether solid thinking is a laborious act should consult a minister who is diligently preparing for a pressing preaching engagement. The act of prayerful reflection needed to move from a blank sheet of paper to the creation of an engaging sermon can feel like moving a load of bricks.

My commitment to the pragmatic has deep roots in autobiography. Prior to joining a divinity school faculty I served as the senior pastor of a congregation in downtown Baltimore for five wonderful and challenging years. Though my teaching ministry has taken me out of the pastorate, I still claim and celebrate a pastoral identity. As the cliché goes, you can take the person out of the pastorate, but you cannot take the pastorate out of the person. At heart I am still a pastor who happens to teach preaching and biblical studies in a divinity school setting.

Pastoral leadership is one of the most rewarding vocations. Yet the process of journeying with, leading along, and learning from a congregation in its quest for the sacred presents constant and considerable challenges to the pastoral leader. So intense, at times, are those challenges that I count a year of pastoral work according to "dog arithmetic." Veterinarians tell us that one year for a dog is supposed to equal seven human years. Similarly, so comprehensive and complex was my pastoral work that I believed each of my five years should have counted for seven years of experience.[5] Consequently, even though I am in my midthirties, I have served as a pastor for thirty-five years. (You do the math!)

In no way is the author of this book ignorant of or unsympathetic to the joys and sorrows of wearing the pastoral mantle. I know what it is to preach to a congregation twice on Sunday, amid the funerals, hospital visitations, staff meetings, and the malfunction of the church's furnace that usually occurs during the first cold Sunday in the fall. My presence in the university's "ivory tower" has not created any amnesia concerning the "grass roots" of pastoral ministry.

Pastors who are passionately involved in the acts and arts of Christian ministry are no less reflective than university scholars. For example, finding the right words to say at a funeral requires no less intellectual work than dissecting a Greek verb. Having spent time in a pastorate and in the university, I have discovered a primary difference between the pastor and the university scholar.

In spite of their pressing demands, pastors do not reflect less than university scholars. Pastors simply have to reflect more quickly on a wider variety of matters. It should come as no surprise that the Greek word *scholē*, which gives us the English word *scholar*, means "leisure." Whether one's congregation has fifty or fifty-five hundred parishioners, leisure is rarely a luxury afforded to most pastors.

Some pastoral colleagues might read this book amid their incessant cycle of sermon preparation, meetings, and counseling sessions. Desiring to offer a book that incites more meaningful Christian practice while still respecting the time constraints of congregational leaders, I will avoid unnecessary jargon. On those occasions when I employ unusual terms, I will explain them clearly. Moreover, my documentation in the notes makes no attempt to be exhaustive. The notes will (1) cite sources influencing the book, (2) offer succinct, relevant amplifications of issues treated, and (3) point readers to a few resources for further study.

A Book About Paul: A Pragmatic Person

The second chapter will provide an overview of Paul's identity and the social realities that influenced him. In the twentieth century alone, not to mention preceding centuries, there was a staggering amount of scholarship on Paul and his theological legacy.[6] I regularly teach divinity school courses on Paul and am still unable to stay abreast of the books, articles, and Web pages on Paul that multiply daily. I can only imagine how daunting this proliferation of resources is for pastors, seminarians, and interested laypersons. Thus the second chapter will seek to provide a summary of essential knowledge for a responsible interpretation of and a faithful proclamation from Paul's writings.

For those meeting Paul for the first time, this chapter will offer a relatively painless introduction to this complex ancient Christian leader. For those whose detailed study of Paul occurred some time ago (for example, pastors who have been out of seminary for five or more years), this chapter will provide insights on recent developments in Pauline scholarship. For advanced students of Paul, it is hoped that this chapter will serve as a functional "refresher course." My investigation might motivate even the seasoned interpreter to reconsider previously neglected features of Paul's ministry.

The second chapter will entail some notable features including:

- An indicative list of Paul's central convictions—the primary beliefs and commitments supporting his ministry.

- An overview of the Roman Empire—the "colonies of Caesar" maintained by a massive bureaucracy and a menacing military.

- A discussion of the *ekklēsia*—those "colonies of Christ" established by Paul and other missionaries where earliest Christians gathered for worship, proclamation, and fellowship.[7]

In the first century of the common era, the imperial tentacles of Rome extended into nearly every nook and cranny of the Mediterranean basin.[8] The presence of those tentacles was most evident in the urban centers of the Mediterranean—places such as Rome, Corinth, and Philippi. Thus the Roman Empire provided the ideological and social context in which Paul labored to build the *ekklēsia*.[9] In the midst of the swirling matrix created by empire and *ekklēsia*, the apostle Paul sought to provide pastoral leadership to his communities. He was an intensely pragmatic individual. The acts of reflecting on and embodying his beliefs deeply characterized his existence.

Prior to his experience with Christ, Paul was involved in the activities of thinking about and living out the dictates of Torah.[10] His commitment to Torah and the God it mediated might have contributed to his aggressive persecution of the earliest followers of Christ. A revelatory experience with Christ, about which he speaks reservedly in his letters, transformed Paul into a follower of Christ—and more than that, one of Christ's specially appointed leaders.

Consequently, Paul began proclaiming the good news of this Christ and establishing communities devoted to this Christ. Persons in the Pauline *ekklēsia* hailed Jesus as Lord. Citizens and subjugated peoples in the Roman Empire were ultimately supposed to acknowledge Caesar as Lord, even if they held on to their local religious beliefs and practices.

By its very existence, the Pauline *ekklēsia* posed a counterclaim to the sovereignty of Rome—a risky endeavor indeed. The difficulties of trying to establish the *ekklēsia* and the dangers of opposing the ideology of the empire created a vortex that left Paul little time for concerns about theological or doctrinal consistency.[11]

For too long Paul's interpreters—whether they are supporters or detractors—have approached his writings as if they were systematic theological treatises. Though filled with theology, Paul's Letters make no claim to theological consistency. As pastoral communications mediating his presence and teachings, the letters were designed to create theological commitment among his converts.

Just as it would be a mistake to consider Paul's Letters "systematic theology," so too it would be incorrect to consider them recklessly written "notes," absent of rhetorical insight and polish. In

spite of Paul's confession about lacking rhetorical expertise
(1 Cor. 2:4 and 2 Cor. 11:6), his letters reflect substantive knowledge of and careful attention to rhetoric, the art of persuasion.

Whether Paul wrote to persuade converts to contribute to a
financial collection for other Christians or to correct perceived
problems in a community, he aimed to motivate persons to appropriate actions in light of the gospel. As an apostle working to
build the *ekklēsia* in the midst of the real and present dangers of
the empire, neither theological consistency nor rhetorical aptitude was an end unto itself. For Paul the pragmatist, the end was
that his ministry and the communities that bore witness to it
would be a pleasing offering to God at the final judgment (1 Cor.
4:5 and 1 Thess. 2:19-20).

Admittedly, it is risky to refer to Paul as a "pragmatist" because
of the negative connotations this term evokes among various
people. For some a "pragmatist" is a person who lacks conscience
and manipulates people and circumstances to accomplish selfish
goals. For me such a description is more applicable to an "oppor-
tunist" than to a "pragmatist."

Paul did not lack conscience. His ministry was governed by a
driving sense of accountability to God—the legitimate expectation of having "to give an account, an explanation, or a justification [to God] for a deed or an attitude." [12] Moreover, his goals had
an intensely *communal* orientation. Contrary to some interpretations, Paul was not the champion for "personal salvation," a
phrase frequently employed among many modern-day Christians.

Undoubtedly, he believed that there was a personal dimension
to accepting the gospel—the liberating story of God's loving
involvement with the world, which reaches its climax in Jesus
Christ. Yet Paul's chief concern was the present and future well-
being of his congregations. He possessed theologically rooted
convictions by which he judged himself. He placed these convictions in the service of building community. Was Paul an oppor-
tunist? Hardly!

Paul was a pragmatist, however, in his realization that humans'
deepest convictions and aspirations often manifest themselves
through action and behavior. As Donald Juel suggested, Paul rec-

ognized that the truth of the gospel was embedded in congregational practices such as baptism and the Lord's Supper.[13] Juel's suggestion prompted me to think afresh about the central role that congregational practices played in Paul's ministry and letters. An indicative list of the congregational practices in the "authentic" Pauline Letters[14] might include:

- Hospitality (Romans 12–14)

- The Lord's Supper (1 Corinthians 11)

- Congregational reconciliation (2 Corinthians 2)

- Baptism (Galatians 3)

- Prayer (Philippians 4)

- Pastoral counseling (1 Thessalonians 4)

- Social justice advocacy (Philemon)

Paul the apostle, pastor, and pragmatist believed that the gospel was not an abstract concept but a powerful event embodied through practice. Undoubtedly, each of the practices noted above could be explored more fully with respect to Paul's Letters. There is one practice not mentioned above that occupied much of Paul's ministry. This practice will also occupy the bulk of the book's third chapter—*preaching!*

Preaching Paul: Paul as a Messenger of the Gospel

Admittedly the book's title *Preaching Paul* is ambiguous. Said one way, the word *preaching* is a "verbal adjective" describing Paul, and Paul is the subject. In other words, Paul was a person whose ministry was defined by preaching. Colloquially one might express the first meaning by saying, "The apostle Paul surely was a *preaching* man!"

Preaching Paul, however, can be said another way with another meaning. In this second way, the word *preaching* is a "verbal noun" specifying an action done to Paul who is now an "object." In other words, the contemporary minister preaches by employing Paul (or Paul's Letters). One might express the second meaning by declaring, "This Sunday my preaching will come from Paul (or Paul's Letters)." In the second way, preaching is the subject and Paul is the object. Chapters 3 through 5 will explore these two ways of articulating *Preaching Paul*.

In chapter 3, I will investigate Paul as a "subject" and gospel messenger in his own right. Even a glance at his Letters reveals the importance he placed upon Christian proclamation. To return to my colloquial phrase above, the third chapter will affirm that the apostle Paul surely was a "preaching man." In this chapter I will examine the implications of Paul's statements about proclamation for our own preaching ministries. Paul's ancient observations about preaching might provide indispensable wisdom for twenty-first-century preachers.

Methodologically I will employ "devotional interpretation," also known as *lectio divina*. Devotional interpretation is a time-honored method of seeking contemporary spiritual experiences with biblical texts by deeply meditating upon them.[15] As a complement to, not a replacement of, traditional academic interpretive practices, devotional interpretation reminds us that the Bible does not belong exclusively to scholars. Before the Bible was a book in the university it was and remains a book for the church.

My partiality for devotional interpretation in chapter 3 is appropriate for still another reason. The Holy Spirit was a central reality in Paul's life and Letters. In Paul's Letters we are still centuries away from a full-blown doctrine of the Trinity. Nevertheless, Paul evidently believed that there were facets or agents within God's being who demonstrated particular characteristics or carried out particular functions (2 Cor. 13:13).

For Paul, Jesus Christ revealed God, participated in God's divinity, and played the central role in the redemption of the world.

Similarly, the Holy Spirit revealed God, participated in God's divinity, and played the pivotal role in empowering believers to embody the truths of the gospel, personally and communally. From a Pauline perspective the Spirit is the movement of God that facilitates Christian practice and enables the church to be the church.

Typically scholars have disregarded Paul's significant emphasis on the Spirit,[16] preferring to focus their attention on his understanding of Jesus. Yet Paul insisted that the work of the Spirit, which was an extension of Christ's work, was an indispensable ingredient for the church. For Paul, "the Spirit [was] truly God in action."[17]

Preaching was a decisive Christian practice in which the Holy Spirit was operative. Apart from the Spirit preaching mutated into mere human words (1 Thess. 1:5). As the Spirit played a key role in Paul's preaching, so too we will invite the Spirit to be our guide as we investigate Paul's ancient statements about preaching for our contemporary preaching ministries.

Preaching Paul: Paul's Letters in Service of the Gospel

Having explored the ancient preaching of Paul in chapter 3, I explore in chapters 4 and 5 how contemporary preachers can employ Paul's Letters in gospel proclamation. Chapter 4 will focus on effective methods of *homiletical* biblical interpretation. Chapter 5 will examine various theological and rhetorical aspects of effective preaching from Paul's Letters.

One can have a variety of legitimate goals when reading the Bible. Our interpretive intentions greatly influence our interpretive procedures. [18] For example, some read biblical texts expecting them to assist in the historical reconstruction of the ancient authors and communities behind those texts. Others read biblical texts expecting them to provide insights for contemporary cultural analysis and critique.

Preachers, however, go to biblical texts with a mandate from their communities to bring back the gospel—a probing word about God, and even from God, which speaks to the deepest issues of existence. This communal expectation that the Bible figures prominently in the proclamation of the gospel distinguishes biblical interpretation for preaching from certain other traditional academic interpretations of the Bible. Though homiletical readings of the Bible ought to deal with ancient historical realities and contemporary cultural critique, homiletical interpretations ultimately must be theological and *evangelical*.

Unfortunately, in many contemporary settings the term *evangelical* has almost become a dirty word. The word conjures problematic images of a type of Christianity that is ultra-rightwing and exclusionary in its theological and political practices. My use of the word *evangelical* does not specify any particular segment or denomination within the church. Rather, I use the term in the literal sense of the Greek word from which it is derived, *euangelion*. The word means "good announcement," "good news," or simply "gospel." Broadly speaking, every Christian community and every preacher should be evangelical in the sense that they are striving, however imperfectly, to bear witness to the gospel.

Thus preachers have not fulfilled their tasks if their sermons simply expose listeners to a history lesson on the text or a cultural critique of the text in light of the most fashionable ideological positions. As important as various historical and cultural interpretative practices are, preachers finally converse with biblical texts, searching for the light those texts might shine upon the gospel.

In my estimation, it is a mistake to equate uncritically biblical texts with the gospel. The Bible can be, and quite often is, a powerful witness to the gospel. But the gospel is more than simply the Bible! Certain biblical texts, which either promote oppression or refuse to thoroughly denounce it, are hardly good news. Yet in the hands of a Spirit-led preacher even problematic biblical texts have evangelical potential. By creatively reading against or opposing such texts preachers can pronounce the good news that contemporary communities are no longer willing to share in the complicity of ancient oppressions. According to Richard Lischer, homiletical biblical interpretation requires a "theological imagination," which permits a preacher "to read texts in such a way that they will be allowed to release their witness to Jesus Christ."[19]

Conversing with my description of preaching in chapter 1, I will explore in chapter 5 some theological and rhetorical aspects of creating a sermon from the Pauline Letters. A major premise of chapter 5 is that preaching the gospel involves much more than responsible interpretation of the Bible. Without a consideration of broader theological and rhetorical issues, a sermon will function as a religious essay that simply informs, rather than as a proclamation that informs *and transforms* its hearers.

I demonstrate the importance of theological and rhetorical features in preaching by analyzing my own creative process that led to a sermon from a Pauline Letter. Chapter 5 closes with the manuscripts of two other sermons that I have preached from Pauline texts, along with colleagues' critical reflections on those sermons. By including the comments of colleagues, I am modeling the importance of dialogue and feedback in the homiletical process.

In chapter 6, I provide readers with a bibliographic guide for preaching Paul. This guide lists useful commentaries and resources for interpreting and preaching from Pauline texts. It also provides an annotated bibliography of twenty important scholarly studies on Paul from the last fifty years. At book's end I trust that readers will be more knowledgeable about preaching and about Paul, and more confident about preaching from Paul.

As mentioned, chapter 1 will present a description of preaching. Before proceeding to that description, let us take what they call in basketball a "twenty-second time-out."

Instead of calling a full-blown time-out that completely interrupts the momentum of the game, basketball coaches occasionally call a twenty-second time-out. This shorter time-out briefly breaks the game's flow so that a coach might provide a quick insight to the team. In the brief "twenty-second time-out" between this introduction and chapter 1, I will explain (especially to the unconvinced) why contemporary ministers should preach from Paul's Letters.

A Twenty-second Time-out: Why Preach from Paul?

Given the controversy that the apostle Paul has engendered throughout Christian history, I need to offer a brief apology as this book begins. I use the term *apology* in the sense of its Greek antecedent *apologia*—an explanation of one's actions and beliefs.

Ministers have inevitably posed a pressing question to me: Why preach from Paul? Many ministers assume that Paul is difficult to understand, overly opinionated, and supportive of, if not directly responsible for, various kinds of oppression in the church. Consequently, some preachers prefer not to drag the baggage surrounding Paul into their pulpits.

These contemporary assumptions about Paul, though understandable, might be inaccurate or at least ill conceived. Some of the baggage that we think belongs to Paul might actually have other people's names on it, maybe even our names. There are some obstacles, real and perceived, to preaching from the Pauline Letters, which I will address momentarily. First, let me offer three reasons why preachers should employ those letters in their proclamation.

The Opportunities

Paul's ministry and letters were cross-cultural.

Paul believed that the return of Jesus Christ was imminent. In the waning days prior to that return, he devoted himself to creating multiethnic communities that worshiped Christ, the *ekklēsia*. Before encountering Christ Paul was a Jew bent on cleansing Israel from its Gentile domination. Israel was meant to have but one ruler, the one God! After encountering Christ Paul was a Jew who spent the remainder of his life committed to "race relations." He struggled passionately to bring harmony among Jews and Gentiles under the banner of the one God and that God's Messiah.

For centuries many persons have read Paul through the lens of the sixteenth-century religious reformer Martin Luther. Those interpreters influenced by Luther have argued that Paul's primary concern was "justification by faith." This doctrine claims that belief in Jesus Christ (and not the observance of the Torah) restores the individual's broken relationship with God. Interpreted through the lens of justification by faith, Paul's Letters seem to focus on how the *individual* is saved from a sinful existence.

Recently many interpretations of Paul's Letters have de-emphasized justification by faith. Instead these readings have stressed the social, communal realities in his Letters. For instance, some Pauline scholars have noted that the doctrine of justification by faith was not an end for Paul but a means to an end.[20] A major focus of Paul's preaching was that the "Christ event" (that is, the life, death, resurrection, and impending return of Christ) could bring Jews and Gentiles together in unimagined ways. Through their belief in Christ Jews and Gentiles could overcome the *social hostility* that had separated them, thus allowing them to form multiethnic religious communities.

Paul traveled thousands of miles on land and sea. He also spent considerable time during his ministry in the urban centers of the Mediterranean world, which teemed with diverse persons, customs, and religions. In service of the gospel, he constantly crossed geographical and cultural boundaries. A cross-cultural, global perspective is deeply inscribed in Paul's Letters.[21]

Preachers who responsibly interpret Paul's Letters will be invited and challenged to proclaim a gospel with relevance beyond its own cultural borders.[22] Paul knew that a gospel that could not "travel" was provincial and hardly a witness to the universal God. Living as we do in a global community, preachers might learn much from Paul, an early Christian leader for whom multiculturalism was second nature.

Paul was zealously committed to community formation.

A corollary of Paul's cross-cultural ministry was his zealous commitment to the formation of the *ekklēsia*. Participants in the *ekklēsia* would gather in the homes of fellow believers for worship, edification, and the sharing of ritual meals. A church was a community of persons called together by the gospel.

Additionally, Paul's frequent use of the terms "in Christ" or "in the Lord" indicates the communal nature of the church. These terms occur well over a hundred times in his Letters. These phrases possibly connoted the ethical responsibilities of communal life under the lordship of Christ.

When one joined the *ekklēsia* and began living "in Christ," one did not simply enter into an individual relationship with Christ. One also joined a new community, even a new family. Paul's use of kinship language ("brothers" and "sisters") to refer to fellow Christians indicates that the *ekklēsia* provided one with a new sense of identity.

Preachers who responsibly interpret Paul's Letters will be invited and challenged to proclaim a gospel with relevance for communal as well as individual existence. For too long an excessively vertical ("It's just me and Jesus") attitude has typified much American Christianity. In Paul's Letters we frequently encounter ethical admonitions concerning communal life. These admonitions were not exercises in self-righteous pleading. They were constant reminders that people's vertical love for God cannot be separated from their horizontal love for their neighbors.

Moreover, Paul's belief that even the creation was being redeemed might compel contemporary Christians to expand their concept of "salvation" beyond the scope of human beings (Rom. 8:18-25). In light of our growing ecological crises, the church needs to lead the way in demonstrating how persons can live *in community* with the entire creation and its many forms of life.

Paul stressed the link between behavior and belief.

As noted, ethical exhortations abound in Paul's Letters. Considering no area off-limits for discussion, Paul instructed his converts on topics ranging from conduct in worship to sexual behavior. As a pastor and practical theologian he regarded behavior and belief as mutually reinforcing. Pauline ethics are embodied theology, the articulation of foundational theological convictions through lived experience.

Earlier scholarship contended that Paul's moral instructions were simply pragmatic, and thus less important than his theological conceptualizations. More recently scholars have argued that Paul's ethical reflections provide crucial insights into his theology. Concerning Paul's ethics, Brian Blount remarks, "*Theology enables ethics. Ethics establishes theology in the living reality of a community's loving and liberating existence.*"[23]

Scholars often declare that in Paul's Letters the indicative and the imperative are inextricably related. In grammar, the indicative is the mood used to describe events as they actually are. The imperative is the mood for commands, describing what ought to be done. Thus the actuality of the Christ event (the indicative) places upon the followers of Christ certain moral obligations (the imperative). Preachers who responsibly interpret Paul's Letters will be invited and challenged to (re)introduce imperatives into their proclamation.

Contemporary homiletics has often discouraged preachers from the use of words such as *must, ought,* and *should,* warning that such words might appear morally heavy-handed and authoritarian. James Thompson convincingly argues that contemporary preaching could use a substantive dose of clear, didactic, moral imperatives. Thompson contends that many Christians are unclear about behaviors and teachings that are distinctively Christian.[24] If our preaching took Paul more seriously, we might reclaim the value of catechesis—clear, moral instructions for those following in the way of Christ.

The Obstacles

Paul and Oppressive Structures

An honest assessment of preaching from the Pauline Letters must also face the challenges such preaching poses. Paul aroused considerable opposition in his ministry, and persons in his own congregations often sharply disagreed with him. In the twenty centuries after Paul's ministry, the opposition to and disagreements with him have not lessened but have intensified.

Many contemporary groups severely criticize Paul for providing the justification for the oppression of marginalized persons. Some feel that Paul's support of a brutal ancient slave system, his patriarchal oppression of women, and his denouncing of homosexual activity have forever blemished his theological legacy. In Christianity's struggles to confront the pressing social questions of the day—whether it be slavery, the role of women in society, or the presence of gay and lesbian persons in the church—the church has constantly turned to the Pauline Letters for guidance (some might say misguidance).

I cannot deny the role of the Bible in general and the Pauline Letters in particular in the systematic oppression of marginalized groups! As a descendant of Africans criminally enslaved by "Christian" slave masters, issues of oppression touch me profoundly. Theologically, I am a liberationist. I have a vested interest in promoting practices and beliefs that sponsor life-giving emancipation. Moreover, I am compelled to denounce as sinful those practices and beliefs that impede people's journeys to their God-intended wholeness.

The church grossly misrepresents the in-breaking, *inclusive* reign of God when it discriminates against persons on the basis of social identities such as ethnicity, gender, sexual orientation, class status, and physical and mental abilities. In God's commonwealth there are no second-class citizens. Having admitted the regrettable role of Paul's Letters in oppression and having expressed my theological disposition for liberation, I also declare that Paul might not be chiefly responsible for the oppressions perpetrated in his name. Some explanations are in order.

I subscribe to the scholarly consensus that seven New Testament letters were authentically written (or dictated) by Paul. In canonical order, those letters include: Romans, 1 and 2 Corinthians, Galatians, Philippians, 1 Thessalonians, and Philemon. I consider the remaining six letters, often referred to as "inauthentic" or "deutero-Pauline" (that is, secondarily Pauline), to have been written by followers of Paul either during Paul's ministry or after his death. In canonical order, the deutero-Pauline Letters include: Ephesians, Colossians, 2 Thessalonians, 1 and 2 Timothy, and Titus.[25]

In the New Testament, sexism is most acute and the support of slavery most adamant in letters such as Ephesians, Colossians, and the so-called pastoral letters of 1 and 2 Timothy and Titus. In these letters Paul's associates resolved, in the direction of being more oppressive, social issues that were ambiguous and unresolved for Paul. Depending upon how one reads the evidence, one could even argue that the stance toward women and slaves articulated in the inauthentic Pauline Letters is an *oppressive reaction* to Paul's more *liberating action*.[26]

If one brackets the inauthentic Pauline Letters, the portfolio of Paul's social practices and beliefs is complex but not at all totalitarian. Interpreters who slander Paul as an authoritarian tyrant or laud him as a faultless saint might not have considered all the evidence.

My reading of Paul's Letters on certain key theological, social, and ethical issues reveals the following summary. Obviously, each point could be expanded considerably. I present these points as a prelude to the complexity of Paul:

- Paul generally opposed division and domination in the church based on social class (Gal. 3:26-29). For example, he strongly criticized the socially elite Corinthians who were flaunting their economic means before fellow Christians who were economically disadvantaged (1 Cor. 11:17-34).

- Nevertheless, Paul was no strict egalitarian. A commitment to community did not negate the necessity for order and positions of leadership. Paul believed that Christ had commissioned him as an apostle, whose task was to create and lead communities devoted to Christ.

- Paul's stance on ancient slavery was ambiguous.[27] In line with his theological principle that social class should no longer be a means of domination, he opposed slavery and its violence. Slavery, however, was an integral feature of the first-century social landscape. Thus, the well-to-do Christians who often provided their homes in which the *ekklēsia* convened probably possessed slaves. Some of those slaves might have been Christians.

- By condoning slavery Paul would have violated his own belief that Christ removed social class as an instrument of human domination. By opposing slavery Paul would have jeopardized relationships with persons whose support was crucial for the concrete existence of the *ekklēsia*. The complexity of this situation might explain the vagueness of Paul's statements about slavery in 1 Corinthians 7 and Philemon.

- Paul welcomed and celebrated women's roles and leadership in the *ekklēsia*. His Letters identify at least six women who functioned in significant leadership roles.[28] More than likely Paul depended on the financial generosity of various well-to-do women for the sustenance of his churches.[29] Additionally, he presupposed that women would be active in crucial ministries of the church such as preaching (1 Cor. 11:1-16).

- Yet much like slavery, patriarchy—the assumed "headship" of men—was a prevalent feature of Paul's social landscape. On two deplorable occasions (1 Cor. 11:1-16 and 14:34-35) Paul retreated to a domineering patriarchal perspective. On those occasions he betrayed his more usual countercultural practices that reflected his positive views of women and their leadership.

- Paul believed that sexual activity was an interpersonal but not private affair. Since bodies were gifts from God and the location of God's redemptive activity among Christians, Christians' uses of their bodies were matters of theological and ecclesial concern. Though celibate, Paul appreciated people's preference for marrying and engaging in sexual activity (1 Corinthians 7). Like many moralists of his day, Paul viewed homosexual activity as "unnatural" and as evidence of humanity's denial of God (Rom. 1:24-27).[30]

- I disagree with Paul's notion that homosexual activity is categorically an indication of human sinfulness. Regardless of one's views on this issue, I contend that the responsible use of Paul's Letters in the current debates concerning homosexuality must consider issues such as the similarities and differences of Paul's views and contemporary Christian views on the role of sexuality, as well as the impact of studies in human biology and genetics.

- Whether we disagree or agree with Paul's stance on homosexuality, it might be problematic to regard Paul as the "archadvocate" of homophobia or the ultimate and only judge about godly manifestations of our sexuality.[31]

Whether readers find the above synopsis persuasive, its aim is to demonstrate the complexity of Paul's ministerial practices and theological positions. Paul was not an oppressive, uptight ideologue. Neither was he an unblemished embodiment of his noblest theological truths.

Lest we become self-righteous, let us remember that when we read Paul's Letters we are committing a crime of sorts. In certain countries it is a crime to read people's mail without their permission. Paul was writing letters to his congregations, expecting the letters to be read in those congregations. Never once in those letters did he ask or insist that Christians from future generations read his mail as authoritative texts.

These are decisions that the church has made and continues to make when it reads Paul's Letters as scripture. I am not suggesting that the decision to read Paul's Letters this way is incorrect. I am suggesting that Paul might remind us that *we* created some of the problems we have with him by our decision to regard his mail as a part of the Bible.

Though Paul belonged to a different culture and time, he, like each of us, was an intricate mixture of consistency and contradiction, of noble strengths and ignoble weaknesses. Each of us knows the frustration of having people rush to premature judgments about our character. In our dealings with Paul let us not do to him what we would not want done to us. If we give Paul a chance, we might be pleasantly surprised.

A Word on Biblical Authority and Accountability

I have taken the liberty to criticize and disagree with Paul. Such action might appear arrogant at best and heretical at worst to certain readers. Some might raise this question, "By what authority do you muster the audacity to argue with the Bible?" The audacity to argue with the Bible is my working definition of biblical authority. To say that the Bible has authority in my life is to say that it is a text with which I must struggle and not always agree.

As I—and the communities to which I belong—interpret the Bible, I will respect its history, and I want the Bible to respect my history. Likewise, I acknowledge the real possibility that interaction with the Bible might positively alter my future. However, the Bible must also acknowledge the real possibility that my interaction with it might positively alter its future. Many Christians assume that the Bible is supposed to hold us accountable to live the gospel. Is it not possible that God also expects us to hold the Bible accountable—accountable to being, through our interpretations of it, an ever more genuine witness to the gospel?

For me, a central truth of the gospel is that God has prepared a glorious future for the creation. As Paul declares, "If anyone is in Christ, there is a new creation" (2 Cor. 5:17). I trust this book's investigation of preaching and of Paul will assist God in creating something new in each one of us and, in turn, in our preaching ministries.

CHAPTER ONE

WHAT IS PREACHING? GOD'S NEWS WE CAN USE

> But how are they to call on one in whom they have not
> believed? And how are they to believe in one of whom
> they have never heard? And how are they to hear without
> someone to proclaim him? And how are they to proclaim
> him unless they are sent? As it is written, "How beautiful
> are the feet of those who bring good news!"
> (Rom. 10:14-15)

This chapter aims to answer the question, *"What is preaching?"* A complex, demanding activity such as preaching
requires a multidimensional description. Examining the
authentic and inauthentic Pauline Letters for their homiletical
wisdom,[1] I offer three characteristics of effective preaching.

In spite of its multiple parts, my understanding of preaching
could still be considered minimal. Effective preaching might
entail more than I present. I wonder if effective preaching can
contain less than I discuss and still claim to be an earnest witness
to the gospel.

Insights from Romans 10

According to Olin Moyd, preachers "are just town heralds
bringing the news from another source. They do not make the
news but are the news reporters."[2] The image of the preacher as a

herald or heavenly reporter is rooted in the biblical tradition of prophetic proclamation. Furthermore, this image has considerable popularity in the African American churches that have formed me. Having preached in a variety of African American churches, I have discovered that Paul's declaration about the preacher in Romans 10:14-15 is frequently uttered prior to the sermon. Paul, quoting from his Jewish predecessor Isaiah, exclaims in Romans 10:15, "As it is written, 'How beautiful are the feet of those who bring good news.'" Paul's words function almost like a liturgical affirmation in many African American churches.

Some churches regularly recite liturgical affirmations. For example, after the reading of scripture a worship leader will declare, "This is the word of God for the people of God," and the congregants will respond, "Thanks be to God!" In many African American contexts Paul's words in Romans 10:14-15 are often employed as a liturgical prelude to preaching. In the churches of my youth, right before the sermon I regularly heard this odd biblical affirmation about a preacher's feet being beautiful. Though the imagery seemed strange, those who uttered this scripture made it clear that the arrival of the preacher was a moment of great awe and joy.

Closer investigation of Romans 10:15 has clarified the strange imagery of "beautiful feet." The Greek word in this verse often translated "beautiful" (*hōraios*) can also be rendered "timely," as in the sense of arriving at the appropriate moment. Thus, one could render Paul's statement: "How timely are the feet (that is, the arrival) of those proclaiming good news!" In other words, the arrival of the preacher, God's reporter, is always a welcome event because the preacher has the late-breaking story of God's salvation.

God's News We Can Use

In the twenty-first century, information has become the "god" of many people. Or, information and its retrieval in cyberspace have become "god-like." Tom Beaudoin suggests that the expansiveness of the information in cyberspace causes many people to imagine the World Wide Web "as a metaphor—however imperfect—for God." He further observes, "Cyberspace highlights our own finitude, reminding us that we can never be fully cognizant of all that is happening.... In this way, cyberspace illuminates our human limits. Yet it also mirrors our desire for the infinite, the divine."[3]

A fascinating development of the Information Age has been the insatiable desire for news. Large corporations have based their economic futures and their claims to fame on providing news around the clock. CNN, C-Span, MSNBC, and the Weather Channel are attempting to satisfy our craving for twenty-four-hour news.

Not enough people are raising this question: Does *more* information necessarily mean *better* information? Just because we have more information and more news does not mean it is useful news. In a world where reports about homicides take precedence over stories about heroes, we are hard-pressed to discover news that is beneficial and spiritually uplifting. Thus the primary responsibility of the preacher is to provide God's news that people can use. As mentioned, the Greek word for "gospel," *euangelion*, means "good news." Early Christians used the word *euangelion* to make a counterclaim against Roman imperial culture. Throughout the first-century Mediterranean world, persons referred to the imperial benefaction of the caesars in Rome as "good news."

But, in defiance of the belief that ancient or contemporary "caesars" have had any good news, Christians have always declared that good news is not found in caesar but instead in Christ. God's action in Christ is the true good news, and it is news that we can use.

Before we can talk profitably about preaching from Paul's Letters we need to determine what constitutes preaching in the first place. What is preaching? *Preaching is the faithful, passionate reporting of God's useful news.* Let us examine more closely three defining characteristics of this gospel reporting.

The Faithfulness of Preaching: Cross-shaped Proclamation

Effective preaching seeks to be faithful to time-tested, theological criteria. One criterion that might especially regulate the preacher's work is the theology of the cross, which is a conception of reality that permeates Paul's Letters.[4] The voluminous scholarship on the theology of the cross attests to its centrality to Christian identity and practice. Without becoming mired in that scholarship, I will briefly present what I *do not mean* and what I *do mean* by a theology of the cross.

Contrary to classical articulations of atonement doctrines, I do not believe that the violence (that is, the blood) of Jesus' crucifixion satisfies or atones for humanity's sins against God, as if God required "blood satisfaction." Moreover, a theology of the cross is not the uncritical sanctification of suffering and violence as mechanisms for establishing a right relationship with God. Many scholars, especially feminist and womanist thinkers, have sensitized us to the horrific violence, exploitation, and imperialism that Christians have propagated under the "sign of the cross."[5]

JoAnne Terrell urges Christians to reject the "hermeneutics of sacrifice," which is "the understanding that personal sacrifice in the imitation of Christ" is the defining feature of Christian identity.[6] As it developed, Christianity began to glorify Jesus' violent sacrifice, no longer simply considering it a "once and for all" redemptive act. Instead, sometimes violent sacrifice became a reality to be replicated in the lives of Christians.[7] This call to (violent) sacrifice has often manifested itself either externally or internally.

Externally, dominant groups exhorted oppressed groups to embrace suffering as an example of "bearing the cross." Ironically this suffering was often inflicted upon the socially oppressed groups by the dominant groups. As an example, Terrell observes that the Christian glorification of sacrifice provided an ideological foundation for slavery in Europe, the Americas, and the Caribbean. Additionally, this obsession with sacrifice has enslaved countless women (especially those of color) in a demoralizing cult of surrogacy—a ceaseless cycle of living one's life simply for the benefit of others.[8] In these instances, the cross (or its abusive interpretation) has not atoned for sin but propelled persons into the "sin of servanthood."[9]

In its internal manifestation, the call to sacrifice has led many Christians to visit upon themselves all manner of suffering in an effort to replicate the suffering of Christ. Julie Hopkins cites chilling examples of women in Christian history enduring unspeakable, self-inflicted violence as a means to atone for their sins in a manner akin to Christ's death.[10] This self-inflicted suffering has often extended beyond the physical realm to include the psychological realm. Some scholars assert that the Western fixation on guilt also has roots in a malformed theology of the cross. According to Hopkins, such a malformed theology supposes that "only punishment through suffering will redress the balance so that if we are not punished by others we punish ourselves."[11] A ceaselessly tormenting guilt has often been the instrument of that self-punishment.

This discussion demonstrates how easily persons can distort a legitimate theology of the cross.[12] Preaching that supports such distortions should be avoided and denounced. Nevertheless, preaching that evades meaningful engagement with the cross and its implications cannot legitimately claim to be Christian. Briefly, I will discuss my understanding of the cross and its ramifications for preaching. The apostle Paul's influence on my thinking will be evident.

I agree with Paul that fundamentally the cross is an apocalyptic reality. This means that the saving dimensions of the cross are located in its life-altering *revelations* and not in its gory details (for example, "the blood of Jesus"). Assessed without the wisdom of the Holy Spirit, the cross is nothing more than a violent spectacle. According to Paul the Holy Spirit provides believers a framework for properly evaluating the proclamation of "Jesus Christ crucified" (1 Cor. 2:1-10). A theology of the cross offers at least two revelations. First, it reveals the mistake of equating appearances with reality. With God apparent displays of strength can in reality be exhibitions of weakness, and apparent displays of weakness can in reality be exhibitions of strength.

Could there be a more impressive demonstration of Rome's bone-crushing strength than the crosses that constantly dotted the landscape of colonized Judea? Jesus' prophetic ministry—especially his temple rabble-rousing and enthusiastic proclamation about an inclusive reign of God—must have appeared to the religious and political leaders as messianic mania. On that Friday the crosses upon which Rome impaled Jesus and two bandits were the cure for such mania.

Christians claim that Jesus' prophetic ministry was in reality an authentic manifestation of God's intentions. Therefore, since Jesus' obedience to God had landed him in the execution chamber, God stood in solidarity with Jesus during that execution.

God was present in Jesus' weakness and death as a symbol of divine empathy for the violence visited upon people who justly challenge injustice. The cross is not God's demand for suffering. The cross is God's identification with people who suffer, and especially those who suffer in the service of liberation.

Thus, in the cross God invests weakness with the divine strength of God's presence. Tyron Inbody remarks, "Jesus' death is more than simply a heroic act; it is, also, the self-identification of God with and for the world in all its frailty, vulnerability, suffering, and death."[13]

The cross does not tarnish God's strength but instead provides a new model of strength. Weakness and vulnerability can be God's instruments for transformation. If this is a legitimate theology of the cross, it offers a sobering message to a world infatuated with "image management." Cross-shaped preaching declares that preoccupation with our apparent images of strength causes us to ignore our real fountains of power.

Economic images and metaphors of strength are predominant in secular and ecclesial American life. Consequently church leaders and congregations have placed an inordinate emphasis upon numerical indicators of preaching's effectiveness. Many church folk would never worship idol gods like those "misguided" persons in the Bible. But have not some of us constructed shrines to church polls, percentages, and PowerPoint® pie charts? Though ever mindful of the concerns of persons in the pew, cross-shaped preaching ultimately never takes its "cues from the pews." It refuses to capitulate to what apparently is palatable and popular. Faithful preaching remembers that in Jesus' parable of the types of soil in Mark 4 only one of the four seeds fell upon good soil and produced a harvest. Statistically, the preacher in that parable yields only a 25 percent "rate of return." In the reign of God preachers who contribute to the genuine spiritual transformation of one out of four people should be considered "successful." God's perspective on the necessary percentage to constitute "success" differs greatly from many of our cultural standards.[14] Faithful preaching welcomes large crowds but does not judge its effectiveness by crowds or their responses.

Preaching that is true to the cross remains keenly aware of the difference between a delirious crowd and a disciplined congregation. The Gospel narratives of the last week of Jesus' life indicate how quickly the dispositions of crowds can change. Certain ones who hailed Jesus on Sunday would participate indirectly in his execution on Friday.

Second, a theology of the cross reveals God's involvement in politics. Those who interpret a theology of the cross as a preoccupation with political passivity, victimization, and violence have ignored the actions of Jesus and God. Death did not rush upon Jesus as an unanticipated tragedy. Jesus must have been aware of the lethal potential of his actions and message. Nevertheless, he willingly embraced the consequences. Furthermore, when judged before various political rulers, he forfeited any chance to avoid his fate.[15]

Paul's words in 1 Corinthians 1:27-28 address God's involvement in politics. "But God chose what is foolish in the world to shame the wise; God chose what is weak in the world to shame the strong; God chose what is low and despised in the world, things that are not, to reduce to nothing things that are." As suggested, in Jesus' crucifixion—a form of execution reserved for the lowest social classes—God demonstrated solidarity with those who suffer. Through the resurrection of that crucified man, God also has promised the eventual exaltation of those who are oppressed, as well as the judgment of the oppressors.

31

Jürgen Moltmann amplifies this point:

> Now the death of Christ was the death of a political offender. According to the scale of social values of the time, crucifixion was dishonour and shame. If this crucified man has been raised from the dead and exalted to be the Christ of God, then what public opinion holds to be lowliest, what the state has determined to be disgraceful, is changed into what is supreme. In that case, the glory of God does not shine on the crowns of the mighty, but on the face of the crucified Christ. The authority of God is then no longer represented directly by those in high positions, the powerful and the rich.[16]

The revolutionary political implications of the cross are resonant in the verb *katargeō* in 1 Corinthians 1:28. The New Revised Standard Version translates this verb "to reduce to nothing." One can also translate it "to render ineffective." In other words, God chooses to render ineffective "the things that are" (for example, oppressive regimes) often by "the things that are not" (for example, persons and endeavors despised by the world). God employs seemingly dishonored persons to dismantle the power politics of dominant cultures. I offer one example from American history of God's tendency to subvert oppressive regimes through persons who lack social power.

In the 1950s, it appeared to some that American racial segregation, which was supported by legal and cultural codes, would last forever. However, Rosa Parks, a blue-collar black woman in Montgomery, Alabama—the very embodiment of dishonor in the eyes of the white southern establishment—boarded a Montgomery bus one afternoon in 1955. In a simple act of courage and protest, she refused to give up her seat on that bus instead of moving to the back of the bus as black persons were expected to do. Her subversive resistance became a watershed moment in one of the greatest spiritual and social revolutions in American history, the Civil Rights movement. As the adage goes, Rosa Parks *sat down* on that bus so that Martin Luther King Jr. might *stand up* and become the great leader that he did.

Martin Luther King Jr. remarked, "When Mrs. Rosa Parks, the quiet seamstress whose arrest precipitated the nonviolent protest in Montgomery, was asked why she had refused to move to the rear of a bus, she said: 'It was a matter of dignity; I could not have faced myself and my people if I had moved.' "[17] According to a theology of the cross, God, through Rosa Parks's refusal to move, was on the move, dismantling "the (oppressive) things that are" by "the things that are not."

To ensure that preaching is cross-shaped, one might pose these questions:

- Does my preaching regularly display God's tendency to demonstrate power through weakness?

- When appropriate, do my own struggles and brokenness show forth in my preaching?

- Does my preaching genuinely engage the real (physical, emotional, intellectual, and social) struggles of my listeners?

- Does my preaching present God's subversive opposition to oppressive political structures?

- Does my preaching support causes that promote widespread social and political liberation, especially among those who suffer unjustly?

The Passion of Preaching: No Homiletical Half-stepping

The news that a preacher broadcasts is so destiny-altering that it demands a passionate presentation. To restrict one's emotions in the name of a contrived sense of decorum is to misunderstand the significance of the message one bears. More tragically, such a restriction misrepresents God, the source and subject of the preacher's news.

According to Enlightenment sensibilities, which celebrate critical objectivity, emotional investment robs the investigator of the necessary objective detachment. Furthermore, in Enlightenment philosophy, truth is an object that one will eventually possess when one divests oneself emotionally.

Passionate Christian proclamation runs counter to certain claims of the Enlightenment. Through their emotional investment in their sermons, preachers challenge the presumptuous Enlightenment fantasy that truth is an object to be dispassionately possessed. On the contrary, preachers declare that "Truth" is the "Divine Subject" who has graciously decided to be revealed in Jesus Christ. Additionally, passionate preaching reminds us that God's revelation in Jesus Christ is the result of emotional investment.

The New Testament indicates that God does not "half step." God thoroughly invests God's self in whatever God does. In Romans 5:5, Paul testifies to God's passionate commitment to our salvation: "God's love has been poured into our hearts through the Holy Spirit that has been given to us." The verb "to pour" (*ekcheō*) connotes an enthusiastic, even extravagant bestowal of God's love, which spills over because of its abundance. God is not stingy with God's emotions, especially as it relates to the work of redemption.

In Colossians, a text written probably by a disciple of Paul, there exists an equally compelling example of God's emotional investment. The Christ hymn in Colossians 1:15-20 poetically praises Christ's role in creation and redemption. The hymn's assertion in verse 19 has special implications for a theological rationale for passionate preaching.

In verse 19, the writer exclaims that in Christ "all the fullness of God was pleased to dwell." The writer did not say, "All of God dwelled in Christ." Neither did the writer say, "The fullness of God dwelled in Christ." Rather, employing hyperbole the writer uses two totalizing words, "all" (*pan*) and "fullness" (*plērōma*). In Christ, *all the fullness* of God was pleased to dwell. This hyperbole in Colossians 1:19 discloses at least two important things about God's passion.

First, the relationship between God and Jesus Christ involves the sharing of God's fullness. Every part of God was touched and implicated in the Christ event. So thoroughgoing is God's invest-ment that hyperbole is the only appropriate linguistic device to capture it. Contemplating the "divine excess" that God poured into Jesus Christ, the writer of the hymn must employ exagger-ated speech.

Concerning hyperbole, Fred Craddock declares:

> Poets and hymn writers have always used hyperbole as not only appropriate but also necessary for the praise of God. The trim, precise, and controlled language of reason alone lacks the size and freedom needed for liturgy. Vocabularies fitted for the boundaries of time and space wait at the foot of the mountain while winged words move ahead.[18]

In verse 19, the writer's words take flight on the wings of hyperbole: God's excessive investment deserves an exaggerated description.

Second, the Greek verb *eudokeō*, which means "to please," is used. "In Christ, all the fullness of God *was pleased* to dwell." This verb connotes God's emotional connection with Jesus Christ. The opportunity to share God's fullness in this way with Jesus Christ brought great delight to God. When God gave everything God had, God did not do it grudgingly but freely.

In order for the world to have a saving encounter with Jesus Christ, God knew that God could hold nothing back. Since Christian preaching is a God-sponsored attempt to create addi-tional redemptive encounters with Jesus Christ, preachers must realize that God's demonstration of passion has already set the terms of engagement. In the initial revelation of Jesus Christ, God held nothing back. Thus preachers, who serve as conduits in the creation of fresh revelation, should model their pulpit behav-ior on God's lack of restraint. We should be willing to give our all for the sake of the gospel.

Authentic righteous passion belongs in the pulpit. By authentic passion I mean affections that emerge from a preacher's own encounter with the gospel. Some preachers prepare and deliver sermons as if their clerical garments are lined with asbestos. They insulate themselves lest the fire of the gospel approach their souls too closely. On the contrary, preachers should want the fire of the gospel to thaw their chilly indifference, to refine their impure motives, and to illumine their faltering footsteps.

One sure way to engender authentic passion is to remember regularly that preachers stand as much, if not more, in need of their sermons as their listeners. Jeffrey Arthurs contends, "Effective heralds demonstrate that the truth [of the sermon] has gripped them and that it should grip the listeners."[19] For many preachers the quest for holiness becomes a professional obligation rather than a personal discipline. When the profession of ministry deadens our emotions to the promptings of the gospel, our ministries are in jeopardy. By genuinely opening themselves to the awesome demands and promises of the very gospel that they bear, preachers keep their emotional and spiritual nervous systems acutely alive.

Righteous passions are affections that attempt to avoid even the appearance of evil. We are very familiar with preachers who use emotions manipulatively in their preaching. Some preachers transform their church lecterns into "bully pulpits." With mean spirits and arrogant demeanors they browbeat their parishioners and poison the soul of the congregation with a debilitating fear.

Other preachers play to their parishioners' sense of sympathy. They regularly begin their sermons with excuses for why the sermons are not as well prepared as they could have been. In this case, the call for sympathy becomes a smoke screen for a lack of disciplined preparation. Both fear and sympathy are emotions with enormous homiletical possibility, but apart from intense self-scrutiny these emotions can easily become hindrances to the gospel.

Unlike computers the human psyche does not possess a constantly running virus protection program. Thus we are not able to screen completely our emotions, whether honorable or dishonorable. Our inability to screen fully our emotions might be an occasion of grace. It creates the possibility that in the preaching of a sermon we might encounter unforeseen emotions that add texture. I would be suspect of preachers who have never shed unexpected tears or laughed at an unanticipated moment during their sermons.

Nevertheless, preachers should be vigilant concerning their emotions in preaching. Sharing one's emotions about an upcoming sermon or even about one's ministry in general with a trusted confidante is a practical way to check one's emotional motives. Twenty minutes of critical feedback from a friend about one's emotional "blind spots" prior to a sermon can prevent twenty minutes of disastrous preaching during a sermon. Responsible proclamation neither half-steps with respect to emotions nor oversteps into the realm of emotional manipulation.

In my exhortation for passionate preaching I am not advocating reckless, unenlightened zeal. I am, however, calling for *purposeful abandonment*. We should be willing to abandon all unnecessary emotional restraints for the purpose of reconciling persons with the gospel. At its best, effective preaching creates a theological Camp David where two estranged parties, God and humanity, can come to a peaceful accord. As ambassadors of this peace process, preachers should be willing to explore the full range of their emotions and intellect to achieve this desired end.

Passion in preaching certainly involves our emotions, but it is more than emotions. Passion is also fundamentally a mental disposition. The English word *passion* is related to the Greek verb *paschō*, which means "to suffer" or "to endure." Thus, with respect to preaching, passion is a mental willingness to endure vulnerability for the sake of the gospel's reception. Passion might beckon preachers to reveal the tender spots in their lives.

According to Ephesians 6:15, preachers should wear as shoes the gospel of peace. When passion attends our preaching, people will realize that preachers place "clay feet" in those shoes. How vulnerable we become when people discover our clay feet. According to Isaiah and Paul, even clay feet become "beautiful" if the preacher is *passionately* proclaiming God's good news.

To ensure that one's preaching is appropriately passionate, one might pose these questions:

- Do my sermons regularly depict God's capacity for "emotional investment"?

- When preparing a sermon do I consider its implications for my own life and spiritual development?

- Do I strive to place in every sermon at least one point about which I care deeply?

- What is the most significant obstacle preventing me from being more passionate in the pulpit?

- Am I cultivating a circle of confidantes with whom I can honestly check my emotional motives?

The Usefulness of Preaching: Portable Proclamation

Finally, effective preaching proclaims useful news. Useful news speaks to people's deepest needs with clarity and compassion. People gladly receive such news and eagerly take it with them once the benediction is pronounced. God never intended the church to be a spiritual Fort Knox, safeguarding the riches of the gospel within its walls. Sermons should place nuggets of truth in portable pouches so that people will be immeasurably richer where they live and work.

Paul's considerable attention to the moral behavior of his congregations indicates his abiding interest in useful preaching. He expected the gospel to exert a pragmatic, perceptible influence on his converts' conduct. For instance, he declares in 1 Thessalonians 4:1: "Finally, brothers and sisters, we ask and urge you in the Lord Jesus that, as you learned from us how you ought to live and to please God (as, in fact, you are doing), you should do so more and more."

In the phrase "how you ought to live," Paul employs the verb *peripateō*, which means "to walk." This verb connotes "a way of life" and can be understood as biblical shorthand for ethical conduct. In his initial preaching to the Thessalonians, as well as in this Letter, Paul emphasized the practical ways that the gospel should alter believers' lives.[20] As an illustration of his concern for the pragmatic, Paul discusses the sexual conduct of the Thessalonians in the ensuing verses. The pragmatic focus in Paul's preaching provided gravitational pull to his theological conceptions, preventing those conceptions from hovering above the daily struggles of his converts. Surely Paul realized that preaching that neglected to provide useful guidance for daily living was woefully inadequate.

Admittedly, we need to be cautious when speaking about the preaching of useful news. Without appropriate theological rigor, preaching could easily diminish the gospel to a list of simple solutions for common problems. Some preachers have become quite popular in the media for preaching sermons that perpetually "fix" people's dilemmas, whether they are poverty, fractured relationships, or physical and mental distress. With routine precision, their sermons—in conjunction with their special anointing oils, prayer cloths, and toll-free telephone numbers—supply the needed remedies. People pay handsomely to be in the presence of preachers who provide such guaranteed results.

In such cases the gospel ceases to be a two-edged reality that makes demands upon us even as it blesses us. Instead the gospel becomes a commodity, just another product for our personal fulfillment. Thomas Long underscores the danger of this kind of preaching:

> The fullness of the gospel may be reduced to those aspects that are seen to be useful in the present. While it is true that preaching should always connect to the situation at hand, it is also true that the gospel is larger than the questions, issues, and needs contained in any particular moment.[21]

A crass utilitarianism has invaded many aspects of American culture. The church has not been spared. A fitting response to the gospel used to involve the words, "Lord, make me an instrument of thy peace." Now some Christians seemingly interrogate God with the culture's anthem, "What have you done for me lately?" My earlier discussion of cross-shaped preaching should serve as a defense against this kind of reduction.

The gospel is God for and with us. Nonetheless, God must always receive the primary emphasis lest our sermons resemble the self-help manuals in popular bookstores. Many self-help books promise healing and fulfillment in the present. Whereas the gospel offers present abundance, it also insists that our ultimate healing and fulfillment must await God's future.

With the appropriate emphasis on God, responsible preaching seeks to address the needs and questions of listeners. But a degree of theological sophistication is required. Some pastors occasionally poll their congregants, inquiring about sermon topics that might interest and assist the congregants. This approach is entirely appropriate and demonstrates respect for the congregation. Nevertheless, the gospel reminds us that we often miscalculate our needs. Recognizing our tendency for miscalculation, Thomas Frank insists, "I don't really understand what most of my 'needs' are anyway—that's part of why I continue to listen to Jesus."[22]

Thus the assessment of individual and congregational needs must be in conversation with the gospel. Paul Scott Wilson thinks that such a conversation will distinguish the "expressed need" from the "actual need." The expressed need is "the need the congregation identifies for itself, in its own words." The actual need is "the need of the congregation as discerned scripturally and theologically."[23] When making such distinctions preachers should avoid a patronizing attitude. Often parishioners are excellent spiritual diagnosticians, and their expressed need reflects their actual need.

There are three characteristics of useful news: charitable, accessible, and memorable. First, useful news is charitable. Simply put, preachers should love the people to whom they preach, even if at times those people are not likable.[24] In that masterful rhapsody about love in 1 Corinthians 13, Paul warns his hearers about the dangers of loveless ministry.

My appeal to love is not easy morality. It is a strenuous effort to hold our parishioners in the highest esteem, irrespective of current congregational climate. People do not have to come to hear us. Even if they populate the pews, they are under no compulsion to pay attention to us.

On a weekly basis churchgoers grant to preachers the priceless gift of their presence. Many parishioners endure hardship and inconvenience to attend church. I tell my preaching students, "Love your people just for being there in church on Sunday!" We should honor parishioners' faithfulness with sermons that acknowledge the real circumstances of their challenging lives. I have little sympathy for preachers who criticize so-called "CME Christians"—those persons who attend church only on Christmas (C), Mother's Day (M), and Easter (E). If many of these persons were to hear relevant preaching on any of these three days, they might return.

Another manifestation of charity is pastoral attentiveness. Compassionate listening—at jubilant wedding receptions and hopeful child baptisms, in anxious hospital waiting rooms, during demanding family counseling sessions, and in chilly graveyards—will provide important insights into the contents of useful news.

Second, useful news is accessible. A church matriarch once told William A. Jones Jr., the celebrated pastor of Bethany Baptist Church in Brooklyn, "Put it where everybody can get it." Effective preaching is at home in the conversational tones of everyday language. According to Warren Stewart, preachers should want people to "experience the Word in understandable terms, symbols, and images." He further observes, "Common, everyday language in preaching makes for *portable* preaching, preaching that can be carried home."[25]

As a professor, I spend much time in the lecture hall. As a preacher, I strive to use language that could be understood in the pool hall. This is not a call for "dumbing down" the gospel. "Pool hall" chat is often as heady as "lecture hall" conversation. Persons in pool halls just have a greater appreciation for straightforward talk.

Third, useful news is memorable. Vivid imagery enhances the likelihood of a sermon being remembered. Effective preaching couches its news in skillfully painted images and refuses to believe the lie that images are intellectually inferior to concepts. Images and concepts actually complement each other. We express our most abstract concepts in images. In human development, our ability to apprehend images precedes our rational thinking.[26] Since images are the foundation for human cognition (note here my *imagery* of a foundation), the creation of stirring sermonic imagery is, indeed, an intense intellectual activity.

Paul's Letters are filled with provocative images. From this we might infer that his sermons were as well. A brief roll call of some powerful Pauline images should convince us of his nimble use of imaginative language: In Romans 11, he depicts the Jew-Gentile relationship in terms of an olive tree. In 1 Corinthians 9, he likens Christian existence to a grueling athletic competition. In 2 Corinthians 4, he reminds preachers that they are expendable clay jars containing the priceless contents of the gospel. In Galatians 5, he urges his hearers to cultivate the sweet fruit of the Holy Spirit. In Philippians 3, he recalculates his religious identity using the financial balance sheet. In 1 Thessalonians 2, he gently cares for his congregants like a mother nursing her children. In Philemon, he considers himself a "prisoner of Christ Jesus" even as he advocates for the freedom of the runaway slave Onesimus. Paul obviously knew that stirring images place handles on truth so that the gospel becomes portable and useful.

To ensure that one's preaching provides "useful news," one might pose these questions:

- Do my preparation for and presence in the pulpit reflect my love for my listeners?

- Do I strive to use accessible, everyday language in my sermons?

- Does the imagery in my sermons make them "portable"?

Conclusion

Dietrich Bonhoeffer, the German pastor and martyr, once remarked, "The primary confession of the Christian before the world is the deed that interprets itself."[27] "The deed that interprets itself" is also a marvelous definition of preaching. Ultimately, the meaning of preaching lies in whether or not it makes a difference in the lives of those who hear it. Whether we preach in a cathedral or in a storefront; whether we use the Queen's English or the idioms of the people, the meaning of preaching should be self-interpreting. When the deed is done right, nobody will ask, "What is preaching?" They will know, and we will, too.

CHAPTER TWO

WHO WAS PAUL?
EXPLORING PAUL'S CONVICTIONS AND COMMUNITIES

> No armchair theologian or ethicist, Paul was a pastor and
> advocate, a seeker and pilgrim, a man of the Spirit and a
> spirited man. He had experienced his theology before he
> ever expressed it, had striven to live out his ethics before
> he ever exhorted others to go and do likewise. [1]

Other than Jesus of Nazareth, no figure in early
Christianity has been studied more than Paul. This chapter explores why this early Christian apostle has
intrigued so many interpreters. I will investigate Paul in his
ancient context, exploring his convictions, as well as the communal structures in which he lived.

Dogmatic scholarship and preaching have caused persons to
form inflexible opinions about Paul, thereby preventing fresh
engagements with him. Certain interpreters already *know* that
Paul is fighting "works righteousness" (that is, the attempt to
earn salvation through good deeds). Others already *know* that
Paul is a misogynist. Perhaps this chapter will encourage readers
to reassess Paul.

One of my former students experienced such a reassessment.
She was very bright with exceptional promise for ministry.
During her second year of divinity school she enrolled in my
"Corinthian Correspondence" course. She brought to the course

strong and clearly articulated feminist sensibilities. Consequently, when she began the semester, it was clear that she was "out to get" Paul. As a feminist, she was obligated to dislike Paul. She *knew* that Paul was "anti-women."

Yet through patient, close readings of Paul's Letters she discovered that they actually possessed some redeeming qualities. Paul was not an egalitarian feminist, but neither was he an evil misogynist. By the course's conclusion this student was able to reclaim Paul as an important ministry dialogue partner, while maintaining her feminist commitments. Like this student, persons willing to take a chance on Paul might be rewarded. The following exploration will facilitate lively interaction with this ancient apostle.

Paul's Identity and Religious Experience

Like Jesus in Mark's Gospel, Paul emerges in his letters as an adult, fully active in his ministry. Paul supplies no specific information about his place of birth and offers only glimpses of his life before he encountered Christ. In the Acts of the Apostles, Luke creatively fills in many of the biographical blanks left by Paul. Yet scholars treat Luke's details about Paul cautiously, recognizing that Luke's theological agenda might have influenced the accuracy of his reporting.

Many scholars assume that Paul was born in the early years of the first century, approximately 5 C.E.[2] His encounter with the risen Christ is often dated 34 C.E. One can only speculate about how he spent the first three decades of his life.

His letters reveal a thorough grounding in Jewish scripture, probably the result of many years of synagogue attendance. Also, he possessed a commendable grasp of rhetoric and philosophy, likely the consequence of immersion in Greco-Roman schools. In addition to his educational pursuits, Paul apparently learned a manual trade by which he might have supported himself (1 Thess. 2:9). Paul's Letters are very sparse concerning other biographical details. Perhaps his life-altering encounter with Jesus Christ eclipsed any preoccupation with autobiography.

The encounter with Christ compelled Paul to reevaluate every aspect of his identity. Before this encounter Paul's Pharisaic heritage had been his source of identity and pride.[3] Paul's experience with Christ compelled him to rethink certain aspects of his Pharisaic heritage. However, Paul never relinquished his Jewish heritage. Daniel Boyarin insists, "Paul lived and died convinced that he was a Jew living out Judaism."[4]

Consequently, interpreters should exercise caution when speaking of Paul's conversion. Paul *was converted* in the sense of receiving through Christ a powerful new revelation that transformed his perceptions of Judaism. Paul *was not* converted in the sense of leaving one religion for another. Also, Paul received from Christ a new commission, to preach Christ among the Gentiles.

Many of the elements in Paul's new Christ-shaped identity stood in some relationship to Paul's Judaism. The apostle to the Gentiles was not fashioned from wholly new cloth. His Pharisaic heritage supplied much of the fabric.

Consequently, a brief investigation of the continuities and discontinuities between Paul's Pharisaic and Christian identities lends itself to our reassessment of Paul. Also, my emphasis on Paul's Pharisaic heritage is an effort to guard against the subtle "anti-Pharisee" and "anti-Judaism" biases that invade so much New Testament scholarship and Christian preaching.

The Pharisees and Paul

Two important elements of Pharisaic belief can give us a view of the life that Paul might have known prior to Christ: belief in the resurrection and political ideology. My investigation will demonstrate how each element possibly shaped and was shaped by Paul's experience with Christ.

The Resurrection

A primary Pharisaic tenet was the resurrection. The Pharisees believed in the general resurrection of the dead and a future judgment. In light of Pharisaic teaching, the proclamation that Jesus had been raised from the dead would not have struck pre-conversion Paul as outlandish.

Upon the resurrection of the dead at the end of time, God would reward virtuous Jews, such as the Pharisees. God would also punish vicious sinners, such as the Romans who desecrated the land of Israel and tormented Jews in Diaspora communities (that is, Jews living outside Israel). The resurrection would signal the dawning of the messianic age.

By proclaiming that Jesus had been resurrected, Jesus' followers were contending that the messianic age had dawned. This contention might have drawn heated reactions from certain Jews such as Paul. How could Christians claim that the messianic age had arrived in the face of Rome's violent imperial domination, both in the land of Israel and in Diaspora communities? Reward and punishment remained to be seen.

Concerning the resurrection, we witness continuity and discontinuity with Paul's Pharisaic background. The encounter with Christ did not initiate Paul's belief in resurrection. Likely, Paul already possessed the belief. The encounter, however, altered Paul's timetable for that resurrection. By accepting the resurrection of Jesus, Paul consented that the messianic age had indeed erupted into human history.

Political Ideology

Also, the Pharisees were interested in political affairs, even though the Sadducees, the priestly ruling class, were the dominant Jewish group in the early first century of the common era. One of the most pressing political issues was the relationship of Israel to its imperial ruler, Rome. Some Pharisees were willing to accommodate Roman rule while others were more eager for political revolt.[5]

For some Pharisees zeal for the dismantling of Roman imperialism and for the establishment of God's sovereignty over Israel fueled revolutionary fires. In the ancient Mediterranean world there existed no neat boundaries between religion and politics. Thus religious and political zeal were often indistinguishable.

Probably for Paul the Pharisee, believers in Christ were a source of religious corruption.[6] This might partly explain the zeal with which Paul the Pharisee persecuted the church. Of his own assertion, Paul was even more zealous for maintaining the purity of the Jewish tradition than many of his Pharisaic contemporaries (Gal. 1:14). This aberrant sect of Jews alleging that a crucified man was the messiah was an affront to God's rule. Prior to encountering Christ, Paul the Pharisee was no religious pacifist. Religious devotion and aggressive action were complementary.

After Paul's conversion this Pharisaic interest in political affairs did not disappear. It assumed different forms. Those who think that the apostle Paul was not interested in politics have misjudged the evidence. As an apostle, Paul might not have advocated for outright violent insurrection against Rome. Nevertheless, Paul's preaching about Christ was couched in subtle, yet decidedly political overtones. There is an example of Paul's political rhetoric in 1 Thessalonians.

In 1 Thessalonians 5, Paul warns his hearers that the arrival of Christ will come unexpectedly like "a thief in the night" (v. 2). He contrasts the genuine hope associated with the day of the Lord with the false hope associated with the "peace and security" of Roman imperial culture (v. 3). Only the Lord could fulfill any hope of peace and security.

"Peace and security" was a term from "the realm of imperial Roman propaganda."[7] Paul's use of this political phrase implied that the arrival of Christ would "shatter the false peace and security of the Roman establishment."[8] Paul reckoned that Caesar's days were few and fleeting. Whether persecuting followers of Christ or establishing communities for Christ, Paul's religious zeal engaged him in the political affairs of his time.

Paul's Central Convictions

Central convictions are fundamental principles or beliefs one takes for granted. They are the deeply held assumptions from which one argues and on which other beliefs are based. The forthcoming convictions are indicative, not exhaustive, of Paul's underlying beliefs. Furthermore, these convictions were not static, abstract theses for Paul. He was not writing with academic intentions.

Recent scholarship has insisted that Paul was a "narrative theologian." Paul's Letters "do not simply offer independent snippets of 'truth' or isolated gems of logic."[9] Instead, Paul's understandings of Israel, the church, and ministry were part of the larger story of God's dealing with the world, expressed in Jewish scripture.

Like actors improvising on a script, Paul's convictions were in flux, interacting with the circumstances confronting the new Christian communities. There was much ad-libbing in Pauline churches because there were many circumstances that Paul and his converts had never encountered before. By exploring the Pauline passages where his central convictions are expressed, we can gain insight into Paul's ministerial motivations. When Paul speaks of the "gospel" in his letters, he has the following convictions in mind.

Conviction 1: The Christ event is central for understanding God's plan for the world.

For Paul, the true and living God worshiped in Judaism had acted in Jesus Christ to save the world. Second Corinthians 5:16-19 attests to this conviction:

> From now on, therefore, we regard no one from a human point of view; even though we once knew Christ from a human point of view, we know him no longer in that way. So if anyone is in Christ, there is a new creation: everything old has passed away;

> see, everything has become new! All this is from God, who reconciled us to himself through Christ, and has given us the ministry of reconciliation; that is, in Christ God was reconciling the world to himself, not counting their trespasses against them, and entrusting the message of reconciliation to us.

Paul's metaphor of reconciliation comes from the realm of family and diplomatic relations. It refers to the overcoming of hostilities that estrange family members and nations. The source of hostility that estranges God from people is obscured by the NRSV translation: "From now on, therefore, we regard no one from a human point of view; even though we once knew Christ from a human point of view, we know him no longer in that way" (2 Cor. 5:16).

Another translation would be: "Therefore, from now on, we regard no one *according to the flesh*, Even though we once knew Christ *according to the flesh*, we know him no longer in that way." The phrase "according to the flesh" (*kata sarka*) is a Pauline idiom connoting humans' futile decision to live by their own power and according to the standards of a sin-infested world— instead of living by God's power and standards. This decision creates a deep chasm between God and humanity.

God, however, has graciously bridged the chasm through the Christ event, and especially through Christ's death and resurrection. God's saving action grants the possibility of another kind of existence. In the Christ event God took the initiative, reaching out to humanity. Instead of living "according to the flesh," persons can now live "in Christ," which is to utilize Christ's death and resurrection as the compass to guide their existence (2 Cor. 5:17).

The cross becomes a paradigm of willful loving commitment to live and even die for God's reign. The resurrection guarantees that God's life-giving power, which flowed through Jesus Christ, will raise believers to new levels of existence in this life and the life to come. God's action in Christ is so comprehensive that it creates a new reality for those who accept it. Consequently, believers' trespasses are negated (2 Cor. 5:19).

When speaking of the Christ event one cannot overemphasize God's role. As important as Christ is, Paul's ultimate allegiance is to God who acts in Christ. Worship of Christ was not a departure from Paul's Jewish monotheism, but rather an extension of it.

In spite of his intense adoration of Christ, Paul hesitates to refer to Christ explicitly as "God."[10] The meaning of God now includes Christ, but Paul does not simply equate Christ with God. Jesus is the Son of God (1 Thess. 1:10) and the risen Lord who has a name above every name (Phil. 2:9-11). Nevertheless, God stands supreme even over Christ, such that Paul speaks of Christ's ultimate submission to God (1 Cor. 15:28).

The primacy of God for Paul created complexity within his theology. Paul believed that people could now see God's will in the face of Christ (2 Cor. 4:6). Yet Paul seemed terribly perplexed about the fate of his Jewish kinsfolk who had rejected the good news concerning this Christ. In Romans 9–11, Paul appears sympathetic to unbelieving Jews, while chastising overly confident Gentile Christians for forgetting their dependence on Jewish heritage.

Interpreters of Romans remain divided concerning Paul's opinion about the fate of Jews who do not accept the gospel.[11] For our purposes, Paul's doxology at the end of Romans 11 is most telling. In Romans 11:33, Paul exclaims, "O the depth of the riches and wisdom and knowledge of God! How unsearchable are his judgments and how inscrutable his ways!" Even though Christ was the foundation of Paul's gospel, Paul implies that God's grace has a depth that exceeds humanity's ability to comprehend. Paul could be both devoted to Christ and leave many unresolved dilemmas ultimately to God's prerogative!

Conviction 2: Christians are people of a new age who still live in an old age.

Like a hinge on a door, Christ's resurrection was the pivotal point between two ages. The old age, which was the province of death and the rulers of this world, was briskly closing. The new age, which would be the commonwealth of God where eternal life reigned, was rapidly emerging. Certain benefits of the new age were already available to believers. Romans 12:2 attests to this conviction: "Do not be conformed to this world, but be transformed by the renewing of your minds, so that you may discern what is the will of God—what is good and acceptable and perfect."

The word the NRSV renders as "world" (*aiōn*) can also be translated as "age," yielding this translation: "Do not be conformed to this *age*." The segmenting of time into two ages was a common motif in Jewish eschatology (that is, teaching about the end of time). Paul expresses his conviction that the present age was evil and full of decay in Galatians 1:4 and Romans 8:21 respectively. The evil and decay were partly the work of lesser demonic forces that opposed God's reign and partly the result of human sinfulness.

Additionally, Paul criticizes the "rulers of this age" in 1 Corinthians 2:6-8. These rulers, including the Roman imperialists who executed Jesus, misunderstood God's intentions. The *self-seeking* power politics of the current evil age prevented people from perceiving God's mysteries. Consequently, Paul exhorted his converts to adopt the mind-set of the new age, which was characterized by *self-surrendering* love (Rom. 12:9-21).

Jewish eschatology likened the emergence of God's new age to the excruciating pains of childbirth. Thus, Paul suggests in Romans 8 that the creation and believers groan in labor pains as they give birth to God's glorious future. When the new age fully emerged, even death, that tenacious enemy of God, would succumb to God's reign (1 Cor. 15:26).

Although Paul taught his followers that the present age was passing away, he had to remind them that the new age had not been fully inaugurated. In the Corinthian correspondence Paul stresses that the consummation of the new age belongs to the future (1 Cor. 1:7 and 2 Cor. 4:16–5:10). Paul's emphasis on the future might have been a corrective to the claims of his rivals in Corinth who contended that they were already experiencing God's glory fully in the present.[12] Paul insisted that in the future

God would conclude the transformation of believers and of the world begun in the Christ event. In the meanwhile, the church was living "in the time between the times."[13]

Conviction 3: To live as people of the new age requires access to new power: the Holy Spirit.

The Holy Spirit, God's empowering presence, was vitally active among Paul's converts.[14] This presence enabled them to embody their new identity as God's elect. For Paul, to be a follower of Christ was to be a person of the Spirit. Romans 8:5-14 attests to this conviction:

> For those who live according to the flesh set their minds on the things of the flesh, but those who live according to the Spirit set their minds on the things of the Spirit. To set the mind on the flesh is death, but to set the mind on the Spirit is life and peace. For this reason the mind that is set on the flesh is hostile to God; it does not submit to God's law—indeed it cannot, and those who are in the flesh cannot please God. But you are not in the flesh; you are in the Spirit, since the Spirit of God dwells in you. Anyone who does not have the Spirit of Christ does not belong to him.... For all who are led by the Spirit of God are children of God.

Paul conceives of two modes of life available to humans: life "according to the flesh" (*kata sarka*) and life "according to the Spirit" (*kata pneuma*).[15] As noted, life according to the flesh is self-seeking and hostile to God. Eventually it leads to spiritual death. On the contrary, life according to the Spirit is open to infusions of the Spirit. Such a life creates harmony between God and believers.

The Holy Spirit's presence among believers was not a one-time visitation. The Spirit dwelled perpetually in believers, reminding them of their adoption as children of God. Jewish prophets had predicted this end-time indwelling of God's Spirit (Ezek. 36:26-

27 and Joel 2:28-29). For Paul the end had begun, and the Spirit's activity was indisputable proof.

There is little philosophical elaboration about the identity of the Spirit in Paul's Letters. The Spirit is an intimate part of God. In 1 Corinthians 2:10, the Spirit is said to search and know the depths of God. Also, the Spirit played a decisive role in Christ's resurrection (Rom. 8:11).

The chief characteristic of the Spirit was power. The Spirit was not a concept about which to speculate, but a source of power to experience. Luke Johnson asserts:

> Language about the spirit (*to pneuma*) and more specifically the Holy Spirit (*to pneuma hagion*) in the texts of the New Testament has specific reference to this complex experiential field in which power is transmitted and exchanged.... "Holy Spirit" serves as the linguistic expression of the experience of power.[16]

Although this power pervaded every aspect of Christian existence, the Spirit especially influenced believers' moral conduct and worship.

In contrast to our modern maxim "Let your conscience be your guide," Paul would respond, "Let the Spirit be your guide." In Galatians 5:25, he says precisely this: "If we live by the Spirit, let us also be guided by the Spirit." A Spirit-guided life would produce a harvest of godly virtues, including, but not limited to, love, joy, and peace. Paul calls these virtues "fruit of the Spirit" (Gal. 5:22-23). Apart from the Spirit there would be no fruit, only moral barrenness within the community.

The Spirit also enabled acts of Christian worship such as preaching, ecstatic religious utterances, praying, and singing (1 Cor. 14:1-25). In worship believers were reminded of the Spirit's corporate agenda. Ultimately, the Spirit was not the exclusive possession of individuals but God's powerful presence stirring believers to communal edification.

Although the Holy Spirit desired to bring believers together, differences of opinion concerning the Spirit created rifts in certain Pauline congregations. For instance, some Corinthian believers valued more highly the ecstatic manifestations of the Spirit, such as speaking in tongues. Those possessing more ecstatic spiritual gifts appear to have disparaged those lacking them. Instead of unity these different understandings became the basis for factionalism (1 Cor. 12:12-26).

To quell the contention Paul inserts a moving hymn about love in the middle of his discussion of spiritual gifts (1 Corinthians 13). If any behavior would typify Spirit-filled life in the new age, it would be love. Other manifestations of the Spirit would become obsolete in the new age. Love would never be out-of-date.

Conviction 4: The Torah, and especially its mandate for circumcision, is not binding for Gentiles.

Paul insisted that the Torah, with its command for circumcision, did not apply to Gentiles who joined the *ekklēsia*. This conviction was controversial among some of Paul's colleagues. From its inception the Christian movement displayed variety regarding Gentiles. Some Jews welcomed Gentiles into the Christian movement, requiring of them none of the demands of Torah, such as circumcision and dietary laws. Other Jews argued that conversion to Judaism (that is, circumcision in the case of males) was the precondition for admission to the *ekklēsia*.

The dilemma of whether to admit uncircumcised Gentiles into the *ekklēsia* prompted Christian leaders to convene a conference in Jerusalem. Paul attended that conference, explaining his conviction to the leaders of Jerusalem Christianity, including James, Peter, and John. According to Galatians 2:7-9, Paul persuaded them:

> On the contrary, when they saw that I had been entrusted with the gospel for the uncircumcised, just as Peter had been entrusted with the gospel for the circumcised (for he who worked through Peter making him an apostle to the circumcised also worked through me in sending me to the Gentiles), and when James and Cephas and John, who were acknowl-

edged pillars, recognized the grace that had been given to me, they gave to Barnabas and me the right hand of fellowship, agreeing that we should go to the Gentiles and they to the circumcised.

Although there was only one gospel, the Jerusalem leaders and Paul agreed to a division of evangelistic labor. The Jerusalem leaders would continue evangelizing the Jews with a Torah-observant gospel. Paul would continue evangelizing the Gentiles with a circumcision-free gospel. This agreement implied that ethnic diversity and Christian unity were complementary.

We cannot know with certainty what Paul thought about the fate of the Gentiles before he met Christ. After his Christ encounter, Paul certainly believed that Gentiles who had faith in Christ were now members of God's elect. For Paul the apostle, faith in Christ had replaced Torah as the boundary marker for the community of the saved. Paul protested against Gentile submission to the Torah. Such submission would be a categorical denial that God had saved the Gentiles as Gentiles.

Although Paul opposed Torah observance among Gentile converts, did the Torah still play a role in the lives of Jewish Christians? Said differently, could Jewish Christians still observe the Torah?

Paul would have responded, "Yes, as long as it is kept in proper perspective." This imagined response from Paul agrees with the so-called "new perspective" on Paul and the Torah. The new perspective states that Paul speaks disparagingly about the Torah because he is trying to dissuade *Gentiles* from submitting to it.[17]

As an apostle Paul insisted that Torah observance was not the prequalification for salvation. But neither was *Jewish* obedience to the Torah necessarily a detriment to salvation. Jewish Christians could keep the law as a manifestation of faith in Christ. A translation of Galatians 2:16 supports this view.

The NRSV translates Galatians 2:16 (emphasis mine): "Yet we know that a person is justified not by the works of the law *but* through faith in Jesus Christ." This translation understands Torah observance and faith in Christ as mutually exclusive. Another plausible translation would be: "Yet we know that a person is justified not by the works of the law *except* through faith in Jesus Christ." In this case, Torah observance for Jews could be an expression of their faith in Christ. Jewish Christians might celebrate Jewish festivals, observe Sabbath, and even submit to circumcision as an expression of gratitude to God and of their ethnic pride while believing in the Christ whom God raised from the dead.

Often contemporary Christians are taught that the Torah and faith in Christ are opposites. For many early Christians belief in Jesus Christ and obedience to the Torah created no religious dilemmas.

Whereas Jewish Christians need not discard the Torah, Paul insisted that the Torah was no longer ultimate. For Paul Christ represented a new, supreme revelation of God. In spite of its benefits the Torah could not provide the deepest insights into God's saving plan. When Jews and Gentiles turned to Christ, the veil obscuring God's mysteries was removed. Believers in Christ could perceive God's saving plan accurately (2 Cor. 3:16).

Along with other key beliefs, these four convictions—the centrality of Christ, the changing of the ages, the role of the Spirit, and the Torah-free gospel for Gentiles—laid the foundation for Paul's apostolic ministry. Still, as a practical theologian Paul recognized that convictions were tested in the crucible of experience. Paul's experience of establishing the *ekklēsia* in the midst of the Roman Empire would provide a formidable test, indeed.

The Empire: Paul's Social and Political Context

The Roman Empire provided the overarching social and political context of Paul's ministry. From 509 B.C.E. to 31 B.C.E. Rome had existed as a republic, which meant that a significant number of people from different levels of society had input into the political process. Democratic checks and balances ensured that no one person held power in the republic.[18]

However, in 31 B.C.E., Octavian—the grandnephew and adopted son of Julius Caesar—would emerge as the dominant political ruler in Rome. Through shrewd maneuvering Octavian would seize the keys to Roman power, including the military and even the state religion. In 27 B.C.E., the Roman senate gave to Octavian the title *Augustus*, which meant, "revered one."[19] It was an exalted title that possessed quasi-divine overtones. The world-dominating power of Rome was now placed in the hands of one person, Augustus Caesar.[20]

The boundaries of the Roman Empire were enormous, stretching north to Britain, south to the African continent, east to Israel, and west to Spain. Augustus and the caesars who succeeded him relied on the fierce Roman military to maintain the empire. However, the patronage system was an equally potent weapon of Roman imperialism.

According to this system, Augustus Caesar, as patron, supplied many extravagant gifts to Rome and other cities in the empire (for example, roads, theaters, temples, and food). In return Caesar expected honor from his social inferiors known as "clients," since honor was the most prized value in the Roman world. Throughout the empire honor for Caesar often took the form of public worship of Caesar. Such worship—frequently referred to as the "imperial cult"—conveyed the clients' gratitude and their association of the emperor with the divine sphere.[21]

Generally, there was no physical coercion to engage in the imperial cult. The pressure was cultural. Appropriate veneration of Rome and the emperor could secure the favor of Caesar's bureaucrats. This loyalty might assist one's movement up the social ladder or at least make one's current social status more pleasant. Just as patriotic rhetoric can be socially and politically advantageous in contemporary America, conspicuous devotion to the empire and its leader could pay dividends in the ancient Roman world. Given the power entrusted to Roman emperors, many persons hailed the emperors as "saviors" who brought "good news."

Sparked by the good news—not of Caesar, but of Jesus Christ—early Christian missionaries such as Paul engaged this Roman world—a world engulfed by fierce competition for honor and social recognition. These missionaries proclaimed an alternative message of Jesus Christ. This message laid the foundation for the construction of an alternative community—the *ekklēsia*.

The *Ekklēsia*: Paul's Alternative Community

Devotion to Caesar was the order of the day throughout the Roman Empire. Yet within the cities of the empire, Christian proclamation formed communities devoted to Christ. The zeal of early Christian missionaries refused to be contained inside the borders of Israel.

Within the first decade of the movement Christian communities had emerged in many significant urban centers in the imperial world.[22] Ironically, the various roads built or improved by the caesars facilitated the travel of Christian missionaries.[23] Also, the artisans and slaves who were converted to Christianity carried the message with them as they journeyed on those roads.

The urban Christian mission certainly predated Paul. For instance, other missionaries had founded the *ekklēsia* in Rome to which Paul would send a letter at the end of his ministry. Upon entering a city Christian missionaries probably began their evangelistic efforts in the synagogues that populated urban centers such as Rome. Also, evangelism might have occurred while missionaries were practicing their professional trades.

After his conversion Paul began an urban evangelism campaign that substantially expanded the boundaries of the Christian movement. He was passionately committed to the *ekklēsia*, the special community created by the Christ event. Robert Banks remarks:

> In the wake of Paul's travels throughout the Mediterranean, Christian communities sprang up, consolidated, and began to multiply. This was the outcome of a deliberate policy on his part.... For Paul the gospel bound believers to one another as well as to God.... To embrace the gospel, then, is to enter into community.[24]

Paul's Letters depict the intense struggles that beset his efforts at community formation. His struggles were occasionally external, as persons outside his congregations opposed his efforts. But primarily Paul's greatest struggles in community formation were internal to the community. There was great concern about how the members of the church were to behave with one another. Another pressing issue was the degree to which one's membership in the church was to determine one's behavior in other social arenas. Paul's community formation was a work in progress.

In Paul's theology the church was supposed to be an alternative community, one that differed drastically from the dominant communities of the Roman Empire with their thirst for honor and power.[25] This might explain Paul's intense frustration and anguish when he witnessed his Christ communities reflecting tendencies of dominant Roman culture, rather than offering an example to that culture. Mutuality and humility were supposed to be the hallmarks of the *ekklēsia* (Phil. 2:1-4). Yet a critical assessment reveals that, at times, Paul himself was guilty of perpetuating the values of the imperial culture against which he struggled.[26]

Despite romanticized depictions of the harmonious early church, Paul's Letters paint pictures of communities characterized by care and generosity on the one hand (1 Thess. 2:17-20 and Phil. 4:14-18) and disagreement and strife on the other (Gal. 1:6-10 and 2 Cor. 2:1-4). A Pauline *ekklēsia* was a living example of social and religious ambiguity. Two aspects of this ambiguity deserve fuller exploration.

First, Paul's authority was never a given among his congregations. Irrespective of his role in founding these communities, other Christian believers and leaders differed with and challenged his approach to the gospel. The turmoil reflected in letters such as 1 and 2 Corinthians and Galatians reveals that disagreement and debate have been features of the church from its inception.

The prominence of his letters in Christian scripture makes Paul appear larger than life. The debates contained in his letters bring Paul down to size, allowing contemporary readers to appreciate the lively disputes that should attend significant religious matters.

Since Paul's word was not always the last word in ancient churches, why should it be any different in our contemporary churches? The mixed response that Paul received from his converts and colleagues should encourage us to pose probing questions. Such questions might include:

- What if Paul has misunderstood the various situations to which he responds in his congregations and he is the only one experiencing crises? Of his own admission, some of his information was hearsay (1 Cor. 1:11).

- Could Paul's opponents be achieving some success among his congregations because their message met real religious needs?

- Occasionally Paul appeared very inflexible. What message does this inflexibility convey about the value of difference of opinion and approach within the church?

Such queries are not meant to defame Paul, who in some traditions is considered a saint. Rather, they facilitate a critical engagement with his letters, thereby reminding modern-day readers that saints, even ancient ones, have flaws and are not above miscalculations.

Second, Paul not only prompted diverse responses from others, but he himself embodied ambiguity. He both challenged and championed oppressive ideologies. This ambiguity is clearly evident in Paul's perspectives on women.

Interpretations of Paul's perspectives on women are wide-ranging.[27] Judith Gundry-Volf offers an evenhanded assessment of the evidence: "Paul's views on women and gender can be characterized as including both some egalitarian features and the all-pervasive patriarchalism of the ancient world."[28] Extended interpretive comments on 1 Corinthians 4, 11, and 14 illustrate Paul's ambivalence.

In 1 Corinthians 4:14-16, Paul employs the metaphor of parenting to instruct the Corinthians on the nature of leadership. In verses 15-16, recalling his role in creating the Corinthian congregation, Paul writes: "For though you might have ten thousand guardians in Christ, you do not have many fathers. Indeed, in Christ Jesus I became your father through the gospel. I appeal to you, then, be imitators of me."

Some interpreters see Paul's claim to be "father of the Corinthians" and his call for imitation as overtly patriarchal attempts to establish his oppressive authority.[29] I applaud serious inquiry into the power dynamics of biblical texts and interpretation, but the indictment of patriarchy in 1 Corinthians 4 is exaggerated based on the social dynamics in Paul's world.

Familial metaphors serve as bookends around 1 Corinthians 3-4. Paul opens chapter 3 with a *maternal* metaphor, likening himself to a wet nurse who suckles children (3:2). He concludes 1 Corinthians 4 by referring to himself as a father who begat children (4:15). Here, and in other letters, Paul does not employ exclusively paternal imagery (see 1 Thess. 2:7 and Gal. 4:19).

Although guardians might assume a significant role in the rearing of children, the father in ancient Greco-Roman families was chiefly responsible for the education, and especially the moral instruction, of children. Exploring the history of Paul's parental metaphors, David Williams remarks, "[The father] was held accountable for [the family's] behavior."[30] Paul's affirmation of his paternal status is not a manipulative power ploy, but rather a passionate appeal to the Corinthians to be more concerned about their conduct.

As with all concerned parents, Paul's call for imitation is not an expression of arrogance, but of parental responsibility. As the first Christian leader the Corinthian family ever knew, Paul presents himself as an ethical model. His model celebrates God's power through weakness, the importance of mutuality, and ultimate accountability to God (1 Cor. 1:26-29, 3:5-9, and 4:1-5). These are hardly the primary qualities of a patriarchal mind-set.

Also, immediately after Paul's alleged patriarchal offense, he provides an example of mutuality in 1 Corinthians 4:17. Recognizing his inability to care for all the needs of the Corinthian community, he mentions his sending of Timothy, a trusted ministerial colleague, to Corinth in order to continue their spiritual instruction. Thus Paul embraces the importance of mutuality even as he asserts his leadership. His assertion might be more pronounced precisely because of direct challenges to his leadership.[31]

In the main, Paul was *antipatriarchal* while not being egalitarian.[32] Though all should work in a spirit of mutuality, Paul believed that there were, nevertheless, defined leaders in the community. Patriarchal culture socialized males to pursue rights and honor at all costs. Paul, however, instructed the Corinthians that in the *ekklēsia* honor comes through weakness and the willingness to forgo one's rights for the benefit of others.

Whereas Paul seemingly avoids patriarchal oppression in 1 Corinthians 4, he plunges headlong into it in 1 Corinthians 11:1-16. There he deals with certain women in the church prophesying (that is, offering inspired religious speech) with their "heads uncovered." There is considerable divergence of opinion about the circumstances depicted in 11:1-16.[33] The fury this text has generated indicates how much interpreters think is at stake here concerning the roles of women in Christianity and understandings of gender difference. Similarly, Antoinette Wire suggests that the great length to which Paul goes in his multiple arguments also indicates that much is at stake for him.[34]

The problem vexing Paul emerges in 11:5: "But any woman who prays or prophesies with her head unveiled disgraces her head." Apparently certain Christian women prophets in Corinth have broken with prevailing social custom by either removing their head coverings or loosing their hair and literally letting it down while speaking in worship. Paul is concerned that people inside and outside the Corinthian church might see that these women had shamefully disregarded gender distinctions symbolized by "appropriate" hairstyles. Additionally, these women might be considered members of suspect social groups whose women prophets also let their hair down in frenzied prophetic utterances.

While fully assuming that women play vital leadership roles in Christian worship, Paul cannot endure the shameful implications of their actions and mounts three basic arguments. He argues on the basis of cultural codes in verses 4-6; on the basis of the Genesis creation stories in verses 7-9; and finally on the basis of "nature" in verses 14-15.

Even apart from a detailed analysis of Paul's complicated arguments, verse 16 reveals Paul's own doubt about the persuasiveness of his previous arguments. In frustration, he exclaims, "We have no such custom [for women prophesying with their hair down]." A paraphrase of Paul's socially conservative plea might be: "Do as I have urged because this is the way we have always done it."

Though I defended Paul against patriarchy in 1 Corinthians 4, I offer no such defense here. Paul's words in 1 Corinthians 11 are riddled with patriarchal assumptions! Underneath the layers of patriarchy there is an intriguing *message*. Unfortunately, this message is overshadowed by a problematic *motive* and a patriarchal *method*.

His message is the importance of maintaining gender distinctions in the *ekklēsia*. This might partly explain the appeal to the creation stories in Genesis. Christ has redeemed the created order. Nonetheless, certain aspects of the created order remain in force—gender distinctions being one of them. Paul believes that Christ liberates humanity from the hierarchical *dominance* in male-female relationships (Gal. 3:28). Christ does not eradicate the gender *difference* in those relationships—difference being expressed in this case by hairstyles.

From a liberationist perspective Paul's message is compelling. Much feminist and womanist scholarship has attempted to carve out space for the unique perspectives and approaches of women in distinction to men. Also, to his credit, Paul calls into question exclusive male privilege in verses 11-12, as he advocates mutuality among women and men in the Lord.[35]

Though his message is promising, his motives and method are unfortunate, indeed. The avoidance of shame and the maintenance of social respectability appear to be Paul's motives in 1 Corinthians 11:1-16. For example, three times in three verses, he uses some form of the word "shame" (vv. 4-6).[36]

Earlier in 1 Corinthians Paul's theology of the cross emphasized that the church finds its honor in what the world calls shameful. It was hypocritical for Paul to become suddenly concerned that outsiders might heap shame upon the community. How could Paul place the cross at the center of his ministry and be worried about social respectability? Surely the social shame of women's uncovered heads was not comparable to the social shame of the crown of thorns placed on Jesus' head. Since Paul incorporated and even celebrated the social shame of his devotion to a "crucified bandit," his agitation about the social shame associated with these female prophets seems bizarre.

Additionally, Paul employs a patriarchal method when reading the creation stories in verses 7-9. No amount of interpretative maneuvering can rescue him from the charge of chauvinism here. His assertion that a woman brings glory to a man and not directly to God gives to women a derivative, second-class status.

Unfortunately, Paul's chauvinism in 1 Corinthians 11:1-16 is surpassed only by his patriarchal perspective in 14:34-35. In this notorious passage, Paul urges women in the Corinthian congregation to be silent:

> As in all the churches of the saints, women should be silent in the churches. For they are not permitted to speak, but should be subordinate, as the law also says. If there is anything they desire to know, let them ask their husbands at home. For it is shameful for a woman to speak in church.

Seemingly Paul's harsh words undermine any understanding of him as socially progressive. To protect Paul's reputation interpreters have developed elaborate interpolation theories, contending that a copyist inserted these offensive verses after Paul wrote the letter.[37]

I believe that the verses are authentic to Paul. For instance, Paul's concern about social shame in these verses is quite similar to his concern in 1 Corinthians 11. First Corinthians 14:34-35 supplies ample evidence to convict Paul of patriarchy. However, I caution interpreters about making too little or too much of the conviction.

We make too little of these verses by failing to acknowledge their utterly harmful effect on gender equality in church and society. Whether Paul effectively silenced the Corinthian women is a historical mystery. These words, nevertheless, have muted many female voices and assassinated many female dreams throughout history. Words so harmful can hardly be considered the gospel, since the gospel brings life and not death.

Yet we make too much of these verses when we interpret them as Paul's last word on women and gender relations. Inappropriate speech in worship is an overarching theme in 1 Corinthians 11-14. Paul felt that particular Corinthian women were disrupting worship through their vocal expressions. Probably these women thought that their vocal participation was spiritual and edifying to the assembly.

Clearly Paul's declaration, however offensive, was not a blanket prohibition against all women's participation and vocal leadership in the church—even if a later disciple of Paul thought that this was his meaning (1 Tim. 2:11-12). For instance, in spite of his chauvinism in 1 Corinthians 11, Paul assumes that women will preach in Christian worship. He simply wants them to wear "proper" hairstyles while preaching.

The vigor of Paul's reprimand in 1 Corinthians 14 might indicate the strength and growing influence of these women in the Corinthian congregation. The threat of a diminished leadership role in an already contentious congregation pushed to the surface the patriarchy latent in Paul. Antoinette Wire observes, "His sharp challenge and threat should not be read as signs of confidence on Paul's part but as signs of insecurity."[38]

In different contexts, however, Paul affirmed and depended on women's active participation in the *ekklēsia*. Thus, before sentencing Paul too harshly we should remember his standard practice of including women in ecclesial life and leadership.[39]

For example, in Romans 16 Paul commends and greets various women who labored with him in ministry, including Phoebe and Prisca. In Romans 16:7, he mentions a woman, Junia, who was the wife of Andronicus. Paul says that this husband-and-wife team was "prominent among the apostles."[40] Thus Paul's circle of *apostolic* colleagues included women, or at least a woman.

Also, in Philippians 4:2-3, Paul mentions two women leaders in the congregation, Euodia and Syntyche. He declares that these women have "struggled beside" him "in the work of the gospel." The verb Paul uses *(sunathleō)* connotes fighting alongside someone as in an athletic competition.[41] These women were vigorously involved in Christian ministry along with Paul.

Both Paul and his congregations were works in progress. They labored mightily to embody the religious and social transformations created by the Christ event—transformations designed to provide an alternative to Roman imperial culture. Hindsight permits us to scrutinize their failures. Our abiding interest in and indebtedness to their struggles attests to their successes.

Conclusion

As an apostle, Paul's goal was to inspire in his converts a deep devotion to Christ. Through his presence, convictions, and church planting he attempted to create a cohesiveness that would keep his congregations together until Christ's return. Until the end arrived Paul's passion for ministry would remain steadfast. Next, we turn our attention to Paul's preaching—a central component of his ministry—and explore its implications for our ministries.

CHAPTER THREE

PREACHING PAUL: PAUL AS A MESSENGER OF THE GOSPEL

In order to learn how to preach Paul's gospel, there is no better teacher than Paul himself.[1]

Having described what preaching is and who Paul was, I will now examine some of Paul's statements concerning *why* preachers should proclaim the gospel. I will merge the modern focus of chapter 1 and the ancient focus of chapter 2 in order to supply contemporary rationales for preaching based on Paul's ancient perspectives. I will engage in devotional interpretation, also known as *lectio divina*, which is Latin for "sacred reading."[2] This is a method of determining biblical meaning through openness to the Holy Spirit and contemplation. Given the importance of this method in the chapter and its unfamiliarity to some readers, a brief introduction to devotional interpretation will be helpful.

Devotional Interpretation: Exploring the Ancient for the Modern

Responsible biblical interpretations respect the ancient historical aspects of biblical texts. Ancient historical aspects include the interpretive aims of the author and the cultural backgrounds of authors and their initial audiences. But responsible biblical interpretations *that have preaching as their ultimate goal* must remember that ancient history is not the only history. Preaching is a *modern* historical exercise in the sense that it speaks to and from the many historical and cultural circumstances surrounding the preacher and the congregation. Preaching is also concerned with modern history in that it declares the diverse ways the gospel manifests itself in the lives of modern people.

Exploring what a Pauline text *meant* for Paul and his congregations is a legitimate task with an *ancient* focus. Exploring what a Pauline text *means* for us now is a legitimate task with a *modern* focus. Ancient and modern history need not war with each other. They can complement each other. Devotional interpretation can bridge the chasm between ancient and modern histories.

Devotional interpretation is *not* the rejection of time-honored techniques and tools such as word studies, historical analysis, biblical commentaries, and concordances. Devotional interpretation realizes that these techniques and tools, though crucial, are no substitutes for deep and patient meditation on scripture—meditation that flexes a person's emotive as well as cognitive muscles. Mariano Magrassi's observations on the relationship between academic study and devotional interpretation are germane and worth quoting at length:

> With regard to *lectio divina*, [academic study] is introductory. [Academic study] prepares us for the vital assimilation that can take place only in prayer. We want to insist on a conviction that is deeply rooted in all Christian tradition: knowledge that does not lead to love is vain.... We all know the real risk of Bible study that becomes nothing but philology [the study of words] at the scientific level, and a pedantic exercise in the cold accumulation of facts at the textbook level. The very soul of Scripture perishes in such research. Surely that is not why God has spoken. But serious study, a genuine tool of spiritual research, can be of greatest service to *lectio divina*.... [Academic study] is at the service of fervent piety.[3]

The devotional interpreter can and should employ the wisdom of academic scholarship. While not disregarding the word of scholars devotional interpreters are more interested in the Word of God, which can apprehend us as we reverently pore over scripture.

Concerning devotional interpretation, Eunjoo Mary Kim remarks, "It is a dynamic process waiting for the inspiration of the Holy Spirit beyond human limitation, involving a penetration of the deep structure of the text through meditation."[4] Devotional interpretation does not require a person to have extensive knowledge about a passage, nor does it demand abandonment of previous knowledge about a passage. Through quiet meditation, prayerful consideration of certain words or phrases, and intuition the interpreter seeks communion with the Holy Spirit. This communion might impart new knowledge, or it might clarify, deepen, or even overturn existing knowledge about scripture.

In certain academic interpretations of scripture *precision* is the goal. In devotional interpretation, *presence* is the goal. A person reads scripture devotionally in order to enter God's presence. When the interpreter reads scripture with openness to the Spirit scripture can pronounce God's word—a meaningful declaration of God's wisdom and will for our lives.

Like any human endeavor devotional interpretation is not immune from shortcomings. Diligence is required in order to disentangle genuine Spirit revelations from selfish preoccupations. The Bible itself exhorts us to "test the spirits" to ensure that the spirit we are hearing is the Holy One (1 John 4:1).

Such testing, which includes honest self-assessment and intense communal deliberation, increases the likelihood that our interpretations convey the will of God. Persons should employ devotional interpretation both to reinforce what they already believe and to be challenged and changed by the unexpected so that faith might deepen.[5] I invite readers of this book to serve as my extended community, deliberating with me the validity of the forthcoming interpretations.

Although there are variations on method, devotional interpretation often involves the following steps:

- Embracing stillness and silence. We must relinquish the frenzied pace and retreat from the noisy places that typify our lives.

- Reading a biblical text slowly, patiently, and repeatedly. The goal here is to surrender all illusions of control over the text and to allow a word, phrase, or image of the text to move into the heart. By placing ourselves imaginatively within the biblical text, we seek to experience it firsthand.

- Meditating on the text and especially on aspects that have seized the imagination.[6] The aim is to connect aspects of the text with memories and experiences in our spiritual journeys so that the text might have present meaning for our lives.

- Praying to God, expressing thanksgiving and asking for strength to embody the revelations that have been received. Prayer invites God to initiate needed spiritual awakenings and transformations in us.

- Contemplating, through reverential silence, the love, truth, and goodness of God.

In this chapter I converse devotionally with Pauline texts to discern how God might speak to us now in ways beyond what Paul might have intended. Through such readings I am not abandoning intellectual procedures of responsible interpretation. Rather, I demonstrate that biblical interpretation for preaching demands more than traditional academic approaches.

The previous chapter provided a rigorous *academic* exploration of Paul's Letters. This chapter offers a *devotional* reading of Paul's Letters that is equally rigorous, but in a different way. Preaching that neglects academic study can become intellectually thin. Preaching that refuses to engage the devotional imagination can become spiritually irrelevant.

Devotional Interpretations of Why We Preach

In his letters Paul does not provide any prolonged "doctrine of preaching." His letters were substitutes for his apostolic presence and edicts of moral exhortation and instruction. He did not intend his letters to be philosophical essays on theology and ministerial practices. Yet Paul was very aware that his primary objective was to preach. He also recognized that the churches he had founded had been called into existence primarily through his preaching.

He expresses his commitment to preaching in 1 Corinthians 1:17: "For Christ did not send me to baptize but to proclaim the gospel." In this statement, Paul is not diminishing the value of baptism.[7] Of course, baptism had enormous significance for Paul (Rom. 6 and Gal. 3). Instead, he emphatically defines his role in the larger plan of Jesus Christ. Baptism was important, but baptizing people was not Paul's main responsibility.

With clarity, Paul frequently announces his role in the larger plan of Jesus Christ. In Galatians 1:15-16 he insists that God had set him apart to proclaim Christ among the Gentiles. Paul might have been ambiguous about some things, but not about his mission. He was to preach Christ among the Gentiles. More than likely the major activity of Paul's life was preaching.

Why Do We Preach? We Preach Because We Must!

To the question, "Why do we preach?" Paul might respond, "We preach because we must!" First Corinthians 15:3-4 stresses the indispensability of preaching in Paul's ministry. Paul declares:

> For I handed on to you as of first importance what I in turn had received: that Christ died for our sins in accordance with the scriptures, and that he was buried, and that he was raised on the third day in accordance with the scriptures.

In my devotional readings of this passage, the words "of first importance" have captured my imagination. Preaching was Paul's *primary* activity. The word *primary* can be understood here in two ways.

Preaching for Paul was primary in a temporal sense. If we read the account of Paul's preaching ministry in Acts, it appears that Paul's initial question upon arriving in a new city was, "Where is the synagogue?" In Acts—and quite likely in Paul's actual ministry—synagogues were major locales of his preaching (Acts 13:13-52, 14:1-7, and 17:1-15).

When Paul was not preaching in synagogues he might have transformed his leatherworking bench in the artisan shop into a makeshift pulpit or preached during a meeting of the *ekklēsia* in someone's house. Whether he was in a synagogue, a workshop, or a "house-church," public proclamation apparently was the first item on Paul's agenda when entering a new mission field.

The temporal priority Paul placed on preaching is indicated by another plausible translation of 1 Corinthians 15:3. The Greek phrase translated "as of first importance" (*en prōtois*) can also be rendered temporally. Accordingly, it could be translated: "I handed on to you in the first instance." In this translation, Paul says that preaching was what he did first among the Corinthians.

Thus, depending on how one translates 1 Corinthians 15:3, Paul might be saying that the proclamation of the gospel was what he did first, or he might be saying it was of first or utmost importance. I believe that the Greek phrase *en prōtois* carries both nuances. Preaching for Paul was primary in two ways. It was both the first thing he did and the most important thing he did from his perspective.

The passionate proclamation of the death and resurrection of Jesus would have been first on Paul's agenda temporally because Paul considered preaching to be his first or chief activity. From Paul's insistence on the necessity of preaching, we can draw an important spiritual lesson: *We should keep first things first on our ministerial agendas! The most important things should claim our attention and energy first.*

But unfortunately, so often in Christian ministry the things that we get to first are not the things that are most important. Most ministers, and especially pastors, need to be freed from the "tyranny of the urgent."[8] Not everything in our ministries that is urgent is important. On the contrary, the important things should be urgent.

Too many ministers pay lip service to wanting to be effective preachers. Often, no sooner than they have uttered this noble aspiration, these same ministers accept several invitations to give invocations and benedictions at various civic meetings. Then these ministers promise to attend every auxiliary meeting in their congregations and also insist on extensively proofreading every page of the church bulletin or newsletter.

In our work as ministers and pastors I am not underestimating the value of our community or congregational involvement. Nor am I dismissing the value of well-crafted thoughtful church communications, such as bulletins and newsletters. What I am suggesting is that ministers will never be effective preachers without setting preaching as a priority. Ministers, and especially pastors, must be zealous about protecting the time and energy that effective preaching demands. Let us examine how a minister might maintain preaching as a priority in the midst of the concrete examples just mentioned.

Effective preachers must relinquish the compulsion to be present at every event in the community. Clergy are often invited to give invocations and benedictions at community affairs. These invitations demonstrate a civic group's religious awareness and respect for the clergy, which are commendable. Wise and caring ministers accept a few of these invitations, but they also turn many invitations down. When turning down such invitations I have lessened my "clergy guilt" by realizing that I have no patent on prayer and that my presence is no guarantee of God's presence at the community event.

Paul's concentration on his preaching ministry compelled him to say, "For Christ did not send me to baptize but to proclaim the gospel." Similarly, many ministers need to say to themselves, "For

Christ did not send me to provide prayers at civic events but to proclaim the gospel."

When these kinds of invitations have conflicted with the time needed for sermon preparation, I have frequently declined them. My reason was that I had a previously scheduled engagement. This was neither a lie nor an excuse. The time for prayer, meditation, serious research, and preparation of sermons is a regularly scheduled, essential appointment on my calendar. I consider sermon preparation to be private meetings with God that can enable public, congregational meetings with God in worship. Consequently, I evaluate invitations to civic groups, no matter how large or influential the groups, in terms of my commitment to my preaching ministry.

In the case of congregational meetings, ministers, and especially pastors, should be actively involved. Understandably, parishioners look to clergy for direction. But pastoral guidance should never be mistaken for ministerial micromanagement. Some ministers will not be effective preachers until they surrender the need to supervise every aspect of congregational life.

In my pastorate I attempted to provide an overarching agenda and vision for the entire congregation. Then I encouraged and guided various congregational groups to share and support that vision. For example, each year I selected a theme under which the congregation would march. One year God directed me to focus on prayer. Thus I constantly preached on prayer from the pulpit and taught about prayer in various congregational settings and study groups. Once the agenda for developing our prayer lives was set, and basic instruction was provided, I challenged congregational groups to incorporate the theme into their respective work. While ready to meet with and assist congregational groups, I was unwilling to involve myself in *their work* to the point that I rendered myself unprepared to do *my work* in the pulpit.

In the case of producing church bulletins and newsletters, which can be vital instruments for worship and congregational care, ministers should direct—not dominate—the process. Wise and caring ministers should offer input into the production of various church communications, ensuring that they are theologically sound and reflective of excellence. But too much ministerial involvement in that administrative process might divert needed attention from one's preparation for preaching.

In my pastorate the congregation possessed economic resources to provide me with an outstanding administrative staff. The staff took great pride in the production of church communications, thereby relieving me of undue stress and time constraints.

Even in congregations that are unable to afford large administrative staffs there are usually parishioners who have excellent editing and computing skills. Often parishioners will volunteer their finely honed skills to assist their churches in administrative matters. Many parishioners would eagerly volunteer their services if that volunteering might afford the pastor more time for sermon preparation. The payoff for the parishioners would be higher quality sermons and worship experiences.

Thus, establishing preaching as a priority does not mean that ministers will neglect or abandon their involvement in community or congregational affairs. It will require ministers to be more discerning about the management and development of the resources God entrusts to them, such as time and gifted parishioners.

Parishioners want ministerial involvement in their lives, feeling that ministers are connected with God in a special way and are God's spokespersons. The belief that ministers have a special connection with God does not mean that ministers are holier than parishioners. In actuality, as it pertains to holiness, many parishioners possess a piety that far surpasses that of many ministers.

But to the degree that ministers and pastors have been called to the ministry of the word, we *do* have a special connection to God, regardless of our moral failings, doubts, and professional inadequacies. To say that a preacher has a special connection to God is not a claim of self-righteousness, but a statement about ministerial function. As ministers fulfill their God-ordained functions, such as preaching, God grants them revelation for the edification of the church.

God has commissioned preachers to broadcast God's word. In order to maintain the vitality and freshness of that connection to God and God's word, preachers must occasionally be absent from other important and worthwhile ministerial duties and assignments. Too often preachers are *present* at everything during the week and *absent* in their Sunday preaching, even though they maintain bodily presence in the pulpit.

Many people esteem ministers because our spoken words might be vehicles for God's life-changing word. In order to substantiate that possibility ministers must set preaching and the preparation it entails as a priority. This, in turn, might involve a reshuffling of other ministerial priorities.

The sensitive pastor will surely raise this question: "Will my parishioners understand and forgive me if I miss certain meetings or activities?" By no means should ministers dismiss the important business of establishing and nurturing relationships and providing pastoral presence. Realistically there are some meetings and activities in the congregation that a pastor cannot miss and still expect to be pastor. However, a consistent dose of biblically based, theologically sound, rhetorically polished preaching can create congregational amnesia about pastoral absences from other meetings. Pastors who are really present and powerful in their pulpits are given leeway to be absent occasionally from other congregational meetings.

There is a misunderstanding among many parishioners about how pastors actually spend their time. How often do ministers hear the question, "So, Pastor, what do you do outside of Sunday morning?" This question does not come from malice, but rather from parishioners' ignorance about our pastoral schedules. But through laziness in pulpit work pastors might actually provide additional reasons for people to raise this question. Rather than our parishioners asking us what we do the rest of the week, we should strive to have them ask us a slightly different question.

After hearing the theological depth and honesty of our preaching on a weekly basis, our parishioners should ask, "Pastor, how do you do anything else but preaching?" What should amaze them (and us) is that pastors are able to fulfill other important duties such as visitation and administration amid the considerable amount of prayer, meditation, and meticulous study that supports our preaching.

A steady diet of substantive sermons will sensitize a congregation to a pastor's need for long uninterrupted periods of preparation—not simply during a summer sabbatical, but every week. Through excellence in the pulpit ministers demonstrate to God and to parishioners that such time was well spent. Often in surveys congregations cite "effective preaching" as the primary duty of a pastor. When pastors preserve substantial time for sermon preparation, and when congregations creatively work to provide pastors such time, the end result can be powerful, life-transforming preaching!

To gauge the priorities in one's ministry, one might pose these questions:

- If I were to evaluate critically my ministry, what activity is of first importance?

- What evidence can I provide of the priority of this activity in my ministry (for example, the amount of time spent, my passion or intensity for the activity, parishioners' comments concerning the activity's effect upon their lives)?

- Am I satisfied that this activity is primary in my ministry? If not, what steps might I take to change this?

- What one adjective would the members of my congregation use to describe my preaching?

- What do I need in order to make preaching a stronger priority in my ministry?

  a) time

  b) resources

c) motivation

d) congregational support

e) other_____

There is an old maxim that states, "Lips will say anything, but behavior never lies." Often clergy state their ministry priorities but then undermine these priorities with their practices. The above questions might motivate a minister to assess honestly the gaps between the articulation of priorities and the actualization of priorities. Are our stated ministry priorities claiming the majority of our time and energy?

For ministers who want to make preaching a stronger priority, I encourage the following congregational exercise. Assemble a small group of parishioners, preferably congregational leaders. Supply the parishioners with note cards and ask them to provide written responses to this simple question: "What are the components of an effective sermon?" Even a gathering of five or ten lay leaders will inevitably produce extremely divergent responses. Ask a lay leader to record all the responses on a board and to lead a group discussion about the time and resources that a minister would need to reasonably meet all the recorded sermonic expectations.

This exercise benefits ministers by making them explicitly aware of the congregation's expectations about preaching. It also benefits parishioners by making them explicitly aware of their enormous expectations of ministers and of sermons. Parishioners might not (and perhaps should not) reduce their expectations of preaching, but they might be more sensitive and willing to provide additional resources for ministers to shoulder those expectations.

In a task as complex as Christian ministry a person can legitimately have several priorities, and these priorities might change at particular stages of ministry. Through various activities such as Christian education, social justice activism, and pastoral counseling, the church proclaims the gospel. Still, from Paul's perspective, fervent oral proclamation of the gospel must always remain atop the church's agenda.

In my spiritual imagination I can see someone asking Paul: "Paul, why do you preach?" Paul might respond, "I preach because I have to. Like my prophetic predecessor Jeremiah, even if I wanted to stop preaching I could not. The compulsion to preach burns inside of me like a white-hot fire (Jer. 20:9). Woe is me if I preach not the gospel (1 Cor. 9:16)!"

Someone might follow this first question with another question: "Paul, why are you so passionate about preaching?" Paul might respond, "I am passionate about preaching because without preaching the church ceases to be the church! This was my point in Romans 10:17 when I declared, 'So faith comes from what is heard, and what is heard comes through the word of Christ.' The proclaimed and received word is crucial to the formation of Christian identity and community."

Let me amplify Paul's imaginary responses. No matter how sophisticated and well organized a Christian gathering might be, a church cannot be a church without the preaching of the gospel. The gospel, which the preacher bears, brings life, vitality, and shape to the Christian community. Were it not for the preacher bringing the gospel into the midst of the assembly, we would need to rename our congregations.

We might have the First Baptist Social Club, or the Calvary United Methodist Community Improvement Association, or the Third Avenue Presbyterian Musical Conservatory, or the Saint Peter's Apostolic Ushers' Fellowship. But we would not have any churches. The gospel on the lips of the preacher—the proclaimed news that everybody can use—makes the church the church!

I believe that Paul prioritized preaching because he knew a vital spiritual truth that today's ministers need to (re)claim. Preaching—the proclaimed word of God—unleashes vast spiritual energy into the world, which is able to transform both the visible and invisible realms. Too many ministers consider preaching a routine chore rather than a mighty instrument for spiritual transformation. Today's ministers are mistaken if they believe that the only ones listening to their sermons are the parishioners in a church sanctuary. Scripture places a significantly higher premium on the cosmic dimensions of the spoken word and insists that invisible evil forces listen to and are affected by divine speech.

In Genesis 1, God creates by the *spoken word*, bringing order to the unruly waters of chaos and evil. In Revelation 19:15, the conquering Christ defeats God's adversaries not with a metal sword, but with a sword coming from Christ's *mouth*. This is surely a metaphor for the spoken word of God. Thus, scripture is framed by two arresting allusions to the life-giving, darkness-dispelling, devil-defeating power of the *spoken* word!

God intends for preaching to influence perceptible human existence, forming communities committed to Christ. God also intends for preaching to influence, disrupt, and ultimately dethrone those spiritual forces undetectable to human senses that seek to seduce us from God. As I tell my students, we should preach with gusto because preaching has the potential to render evil spirits unemployed. Or, to use the language of Paul, preaching can root out spiritual "strongholds" that house destructive spiritual forces (2 Cor. 10:4).

Thus the next time we preach, even if a parishioner on the third row might have tuned us out, the evil spirits that plague the world with greed, lust, jealousy, and violence might be eavesdropping on our pulpit conversation. Dynamic, effective proclamation can send those spirits into retreat.

Why Do We Preach? We Preach Because We Can!

To the question, "Why do we preach?" Paul might also respond, "We preach because we can!" If 1 Corinthians 15:3-4 underscores the indispensability of preaching, 2 Corinthians 4:5-7 specifies the ultimate ability for preaching. In that passage, Paul declares:

> For we do not proclaim ourselves; we proclaim Jesus Christ as
> Lord and ourselves as your slaves for Jesus' sake. For it is the
> God who said, "Let light shine out of darkness," who has shone
> in our hearts to give the light of the knowledge of the glory of
> God in the face of Jesus Christ. But we have this treasure in
> clay jars, so that it may be made clear that this extraordinary
> power belongs to God and does not come from us.

This "extraordinary power that comes from God," which is readily available to every preacher, has captured my spiritual imagination. Because of this power preaching is not only a necessary task; it is also an achievable task.

Thus far, I have strongly emphasized the need for us to make preaching a preeminent priority in our ministerial and pastoral work. An anticipated objection to my argument would be: "What about ministers for whom preaching is not the strong suit? Some ministers are not as gifted as others in the area of preaching." I think it is admirable for preachers to know their strengths and weaknesses, but I wonder whether Paul would have had much sympathy for such an objection.

Though Paul had some training in Greco-Roman rhetoric, he was no silver-tongued orator. A major criticism leveled against Paul was that his sermons lacked persuasive luster. For instance, in 2 Corinthians 10:10 Paul alludes to this criticism of his preaching. His opponents gave him credit for writing impressive letters, but they ridiculed his weak physical presence and his unimpressive oratory. Paul had his share of congregational critics.

Moreover, in 2 Corinthians 11:6 Paul admits that he had limited rhetorical training. Concerning oratorical ability Paul probably fell somewhere in the middle of the spectrum. He was not a rhetorical expert, nor was he completely deficient in oral persuasion.

Thus, irrespective of his personal abilities or shortcomings in preaching, Paul realized that preaching still was of first importance in the overall execution of his ministry. Paul might say that for people to make preaching a priority simply because they possess excellent speaking skills would border on idolatry. By the same token, it also borders on idolatry when persons fail to make preaching a priority because of a perceived or real lack of oratorical skills. In either instance the preacher would miss the important theological reality that Paul stresses in 2 Corinthians 4:5-7: the extraordinary power for preaching belongs to God and does not come from us.

More than likely Paul's missionary colleagues could preach circles around him. This, however, did not diminish Paul's zealous commitment to preaching. In spite of criticisms about his homiletical ability, Paul recognized how crucial preaching was to the ongoing work of the church.

Some ministers are too thin-skinned as it relates to preaching. Wise ministers never totally dismiss people's criticisms of their preaching skills and sermons. Occasionally even exaggerated criticisms contain a morsel of truth. Yet preachers should never cower in fear of complaints about their preaching skills. Neither should preachers be anxious about congregants who compare them to other preachers.

To preachers who are overly concerned that they are not as skilled as other preachers, I imagine Paul would say, "Get over it! My congregants and critics often complained that I was not as good as other preachers. I had to develop a thick skin, and you should too. As a preacher you are not trying to win a homiletics award or impress your hearers. Your goal is to be a credible, responsible witness to Christ in the community where you serve. Use the gifts God has provided you, and allow the extraordinary power of God to make up the difference."

Furthermore, let me offer another response to ministers who doubt their preaching abilities. If God lays the responsibility to preach upon a minister, God will also supply the ultimate ability to fulfill the task. I do not mean that preachers are relieved of strenuous effort simply because God has called them to preach. God will not be mocked or taken advantage of, even by the ministers whom God chooses. I mean that God has given to all preachers the fundamental aptitude for offering to their hearers convincing sermons and transforming encounters with Christ.

But preachers must claim and own that aptitude. Every preacher has the ability to proclaim the gospel.

As preachers we might not have remarkable rhetorical facility, but we have Holy Spirit ability. Inherent in our calls to preach is the ability. To think otherwise is to make God either malicious or aimless.

If God gave preachers the mission to proclaim the gospel but not the ability, this would be a formula for futility. God would be malicious, requiring us to fulfill an impossible task. However, if God gave preachers the ability to preach but not a driving sense of divine calling and purpose, God would be aimless, empowering us to fulfill a task that met no larger purpose. God is neither malicious nor aimless. God supplies to preachers both the mandate to preach and the means for preaching.

The ultimate ability and power for preaching come from God. Techniques to enhance and sharpen our preaching might come from the seminary classroom, textbooks, and practice. But we err when we overemphasize technique to the neglect of preaching's ultimate power source. I am not devaluing the imparting of technique to the beginning preacher or the homiletical veteran. Preachers need to be more attentive to techniques that will enhance the effectiveness of their communication. Also, on a more personal note, if homiletical technique were unnecessary, I—as a homiletics professor—would be unemployed, and this book would be a waste of time.

I am suggesting that excellent communication methods apart from a larger sense of spiritual empowerment might serve us no better than an eagerness to preach that pays no attention to technique. Technique apart from an appreciation of the Holy Spirit's power might result in enlightened arrogance. However, a reliance on the Holy Spirit's power apart from an appreciation of communication technique might result in uninformed zeal. Surely God does not expect us to choose either of these evils: enlightened arrogance or uninformed zeal.

The most persuasive and powerful preaching weds solid technique to the preacher's ultimate power source. The ultimate power source is the anointing of the Holy Spirit. In the language of 2 Corinthians 4, this is the extraordinary power of God. By anointing I mean the Spirit's joyful, generous, and ongoing investment of divine inspiration and illumination in our ministries. Tragically the language of Holy Spirit anointing is scarce in much mainstream homiletical literature. James Forbes addresses this scarcity:

> Many Christians are Holy Spirit-shy. For some, conversations about empowerment of the Spirit in one's ministry are occasions of anxiety and intimidation. Some preachers hesitate to speak of the Spirit in relationship to what they do. Others talk about the Spirit in traditional language of faith, but without personal meaning.... But there is another reason why some of us shy away from the Spirit. Many of us fear being grasped by an invisible presence we cannot control.[9]

Deep, intimate fellowship with the Holy Spirit involves an admission of human weakness, the relinquishment of our illusions of being in control, and an embrace of the mysterious and the intuitive. The term *anointing* suggests a kind of Pentecostalism that causes some "traditional" Christians to shudder in disgust. Admittedly, some persons have utilized language of the Holy Spirit to manipulate and defraud others and to manufacture "religious spectacles" long on emotionalism and short on substance. These abuses must not discourage us from earnestly inviting the Spirit to take control of our lives and ministries.

Paul rarely used the specific language of anointing. Only in 2 Corinthians 1:21-22 did he use the verb "to anoint" (*chriō*). Paul writes: "But it is God who establishes us with you in Christ and has anointed us, by putting his seal on us and giving us his Spirit in our hearts as a first installment." In this passage the anointing spoken of is not specifically related to preaching. Rather it is the general reception of the Holy Spirit that occurs when a person accepts God's salvation through Christ. Although Paul rarely uses the specific language of anointing, his references to the Holy Spirit are numerous. As suggested in chapter 2, the intense presence and work of the Holy Spirit among believers was a central conviction for Paul. He believed that the Holy Spirit was the power of God enabling Christians to live as "new age" people even as the old age passed away. To have accepted Christ was to have received an anointing. So, in an absolute sense, every Christian is anointed.

Yet it is possible to speak of anointing in a more specific sense. God gives persons particular assignments for the edification of the church and community. These assignments demand special abilities. For example, certain people receive particular assignments to be preachers within their general calling to be Christians. Similarly, other persons receive equally noble assignments to serve the church and community in their respective walks of life.

Accordingly, I believe the Spirit has a particular anointing that facilitates preaching. Like God, this anointing for preaching shows no partiality. It is the inheritance of every preacher. But as the parable of the prodigal reminds us, people occasionally use their inheritance unwisely (Luke 15:11-32). For too long some preachers have squandered their spiritual inheritance in the far country of fear and skepticism concerning the Holy Spirit. Like the parent in that parable, God eagerly waits for us in order to impart lavish divine power to our lives and preaching ministries. I insisted earlier that we preach because we must. Now I argue that since we must, God ensures that we can. The ultimate ability to preach is a function of the Spirit's anointing.

The call to preach and the anointing to continuously fulfill that call should induce humility, not self-importance, in preachers. According to 2 Corinthians 4:7, preachers are "earthen vessels." On our best days preachers are still ordained dust and commissioned clay. But for reasons known only to God the Holy Spirit regularly enters and endows these earthen vessels with God's extraordinary powers of illumination and inspiration. This investiture of power assumes many manifestations in the preaching ministry. Briefly, let me explore two areas where preachers can experience the Spirit's anointing. Certain Pauline texts will assist the exploration.

Anointed Preparation

Preachers should ask the Spirit to anoint their preparation. On several occasions I have asked experienced preachers how long it takes them to prepare their sermons. They have inevitably responded, "A lifetime!" In other words, sermons are not assembly-line products manufactured each week. They are outgrowths of the preacher's regular, intimate interactions with God, scripture, and the smooth and jagged contours of existence. Ultimately, the turn of the calendar and not the tick of the clock best measures the time one spends in sermon preparation. Therefore, whereas the Spirit often imparts power to preachers as they specifically study for, create, and deliver their sermons, preachers should welcome the Spirit's presence into every aspect of their conscious and subconscious being.

I encourage preachers to ask the Spirit for "depth perception." I acknowledge the vast scientific scholarship associated with this phrase. But I use "depth perception" in a more metaphorical sense to mean the ability to observe multiple dimensions of reality. In spite of impressive technology enabling us to peer into the inner regions of electromagnetic radiation and into the outer edges of gaseous galaxies, human perception is still quite limited. As the empowering, illuminating movement of God, the Holy Spirit compensates for our limited perception, exposing us to spiritual realities that would otherwise be obscured.

In my pastorate, a wise deacon constantly reminded me that many spiritual realities are hidden to our physical eyes and can only be perceived with the "third eye." By "third eye" he meant a profound spiritual discernment that penetrates beneath the surface to expose the deeper, hidden truths of any experience. This discernment, which I am calling "depth perception," is a consequence of the anointing. The Spirit removes the cataracts from our "third eye."

Interestingly, some branches of quantum physics have begun to affirm what various religions have confessed for millennia. Many religious people believe that the most meaningful forces of existence are basically undetectable to human bodily senses and must be encountered through spiritual sensibilities and intuitions. Now, certain physicists maintain that there are nonphysical forces—*quanta*—pulsating throughout the universe at rapid speeds. Many of these *quanta* vibrate so rapidly that they transcend human ability to perceive them. Utilizing different terminology, religion and science testify to the same truth: there are realms of existence—different states of cosmic energy and expression—that exceed human comprehension and three-dimensional experience.[10]

Long before the insights of quantum physics Paul declared in 1 Corinthians 2:10: "The Spirit searches everything, even the depths of God." The universe that God created possesses forces beyond human perception, let alone human comprehension. How much more unfathomable to the human imagination are the depths of God? The Holy Spirit plumbs the deep places of existence that are off limits to human rationality and senses. More important, the Spirit searches the depths of God, and the Spirit translates and presents to believers this deep wisdom in ways that are serviceable for their spiritual development.

Let me be clear: the Spirit's impartation of depth perception is not an excuse for human laziness. In sermon preparation, the Spirit will not do for preachers what they should do for themselves, namely: pray, study, reflect, write, revise, and practice. There is much godly wisdom contained in scripture, biblical commentaries, artistic works, and the natural environment. As they prepare their sermons preachers should visit all these locations and many more in search of godly wisdom. Information and inspiration for sermons abound.

The Spirit generally imparts depth perception through human effort, not in spite of it. As preachers wrestle with and reflect on reality that they can perceive—a biblical text, commentaries, a poem, conversations with congregants, a dazzling sunrise—the Spirit reveals deep wisdom and assists preachers in making sermonic connections they would have otherwise missed.

Often I have labored diligently on a sermon, utilizing my best thinking and research tools. Still, I felt that the sermon lacked spiritual power. Then out of nowhere came flashes of insight—memories buried deep in my mind, an unusual word or phrase, a smell, a taste, or a texture that unleashed my imagination, or a perspective on a biblical text undetected in my previous analysis of the Greek and Hebrew. By naming these gracious intrusions "luck" or "coincidence" we rob the Spirit of glory. The Spirit was searching the "deep places"—spiritual vibrations and regions in God hidden from us—and translating this wisdom into forms that we could use.

In providing depth perception the Spirit can also implant wisdom in preachers' words and thoughts even when preachers are unaware. In many sermons I have used words, phrases, and stories whose power and impact on others was completely hidden to me, but not to the Spirit. Surely preachers have heard parishioners say, "Reverend, it was as if you had listened to my dinnertime conversation last night. Your sermon spoke to needs I did not even know I had."

Of course, some of the ability to speak directly to parishioners' needs comes from pastoral awareness—the compassionate involvement in the lives of parishioners. Yet again, to make too much of pastoral awareness is to steal glory from the Spirit. In addition to searching the depths of God, the Spirit searches human depths as well. The Spirit knows more about our congregants than we could learn in a thousand years of pastoral counseling. Thus, the choice of words in every sermon is a precious act of pastoral care. Preachers should plead with the Holy Spirit to attach instruction, inspiration, hope, and healing to their sermonic words, even when preachers are not aware of it.

I offer practical observations concerning the Spirit and sermon preparation. First, I encourage preachers to establish a daily ongoing conversation with the Spirit. Since the Spirit is our number one helper, we should frequently ask directions from and give thanks to the Spirit in all our daily affairs. The first time the Spirit hears from preachers during the week should not be when they sit down at their desks to create sermons.

Although there is much to gain from regular disciplined devotional time with God, I do not underestimate the spiritual growth and power that come from praying on the run with my eyes wide open. My informal on-the-run conversations with the Spirit often have a greater degree of simplicity and honesty than my formal conversations with the Spirit in private devotions or communal worship.

Second, in addition to regular conversations with the Spirit, preachers should also specifically ask for the Spirit's guidance in every phase of the preparation and delivery processes. Below, I present a prayer that I frequently pray aloud as I begin each sermon. Perhaps, by praying a similar prayer that emerges from your soul, you will experience a new, more intimate connection with the Spirit in your preaching ministry.

My Preaching Prayer

> Gracious God, give me now the eye of the eagle so that I may see clearly into the joys and the sorrows, the hopes and the hurts of your people. With the bonds of your Holy Spirit, weave my hands to the gospel plow and tie my tongue to truth, so that when we leave this place folk won't be talking about the preacher; they'll be talking about Jesus. Spirit of the Living God, fall fresh on us. This I ask in the matchless name of the Lord Christ. Amen.

A third suggestion is that preachers need to be careful about inviting the Spirit into their preparation because the Spirit will respond. But the Spirit often responds at odd times in order to test the sincerity of our invitations. Throughout my preaching ministry the Spirit has had the mysterious habit of interrupting my sleep, usually around two or three o'clock in the morning. When those promptings have come I have arisen and captured them in writing. I also encourage my preaching students to keep a small notepad by their beds. Some preachers forfeit much pulpit power because they value sleep more than a revelation from the Spirit. As the saying goes, be careful what you pray for because you just might get it.

A fourth suggestion is that preachers should not grow bitter or angry during those seasons when the Spirit intentionally makes preaching more difficult. As ironic as it might seem, there are times in our ministries when the Spirit aids our agenda, and more important God's agenda, by intensifying our sermonic struggles. My preaching mentors refer to these stretches of homiletical barrenness as "dry country," that place where the running streams of inspiration evaporate and poetic images are as elusive as shimmering oases.

For various reasons every preacher will visit dry country, and most preachers will be repeat visitors. But not every sojourn in dry country is the result of personal failure or demonic attack. Quite often the Spirit carefully plans our itineraries for dry country. Surely you have not forgotten the intriguing beginning of Jesus' ministry in Mark's Gospel. We learn that the Holy Spirit drove Jesus into the desert—dry country (Mark 1:12). Certainly, while in dry country, the demonic tried to assault Jesus, but the Spirit had sent Jesus there. If Jesus could not escape a Spirit-led trip to dry country, why should preachers expect exemption?

Dry country is not the result of a sadistic impulse in God that takes delight in our struggles. Instead, God knows that dry country is an especially effective teacher that can provide ministry-enhancing lessons for willing pupils. Preachers fixated on the mirage of their "professional image" usually miss the lessons of dry country. They become bitter and angry and permit the fatigue induced by dry country to drive them into inappropriate and destructive behaviors.

But when preachers are as concerned about their spiritual development as their professional performance, they can patiently—though painfully—change the focus from themselves to God. Thus, the question in dry country shifts from "Why am I struggling to do this?" to "God, what are you creating me to be through this?"

Dry country teaches genuine humility—not the fake humility that most preachers have perfected. The word *humility* is closely related to the Latin word *humus*, which means "ground" or "earth." No matter how *fluid* our tongues might have been on other occasions, there is nothing like dry country to remind us that we are *dust*, and to the dust we shall return. Paul might say that dry country impresses upon our hearers and upon us that we are *earthen* vessels.

Dry country also reminds us that serious preaching is always costly, exacting great toil and tolls from the preacher. When I listen to some preachers, their sermons seem far too "cheap." Like mass-produced trinkets at a souvenir shop, their sermons bear no signs of handcrafted labor or of hand-to-hand struggle with the problematic aspects of spiritual life. Every sentence in their sermons comes with a vacuum-packed certainty that would never allow any doubt—not to mention desert dust—to enter.

But sermons that have come through dry country cannot help but have doubt in them and dust on them. Perhaps doubt and dust often reveal more truths about our spiritual journeys than polish and prepackaging ever could. Jesus—and the God he served—had heightened experiences of doubt and dust on Good Friday! Thus, the Spirit's intensification of our struggles in sermon creation and delivery is a kind of anointed preparation in its own right. It better prepares preachers to understand and interpret for their hearers and for themselves the shadowy sides of spiritual life.

In addition to asking the Spirit to anoint their preparation, preachers should seek the Spirit's anointing in another crucial area.

Anointed Reception

Preachers should also ask the Spirit to anoint the reception of sermons. Often ministers approach preaching as if it is a monologue.

But a preacher is not a "sage on the stage," possessing the keys to unlock all spiritual truths. A preacher is engaged in a dialogue with God and the congregation.

By congregation I mean an assembly of believers gathered in a particular moment and specific locale. Though a congregation might gather for many reasons, the primary motivation drawing a congregation together is a communal willingness to submit to the story and practices of Christian faith. In the preaching moment, a congregation is not a passive recipient of a sermon, but rather a vitally important actor in the sacred drama. The very gathering of the congregation in worship is an invitation to the preacher to tell the ancient Christian story in a new way.

So, a congregation first calls to a preacher to offer a sermon. A preacher responds with a sermon. A preacher's sermon itself is a call to a congregation to experience God anew, and a congregation responds to that call. The congregation calls. The preacher responds. The preacher calls. The congregation responds.

This "call and response" pattern is explicit and vocal in many African American congregations. I argue, however, that the call and response pattern should be *implicit* in the interaction between any preacher and congregation, irrespective of ethnic and denominational heritage. Christian proclamation is inherently an antiphonal chorus between a congregation and a preacher. Thus, preachers should be as concerned about a sermon's reception as they are about its conception.

Paul alludes to the importance of preaching's reception in Romans 10:17: "So faith comes from what is heard, and what is heard comes through the word of Christ." The logic of Romans 10 is that in order for people to receive the gospel, preachers must proclaim it. And in order for preachers to proclaim the gospel, they must be sent.

God has enabled both conditions to be met. God has sent preachers, and preachers have proclaimed the gospel. The uncertain variable is whether people will receive what is proclaimed. I tell my preaching students that the space between the preacher's lips and the listener's ears is filled with heavenly possibilities and hellish dangers. For preachers to invite the Spirit into sermon preparation while leaving the sermon's reception to the whims of the moment is irresponsible at best and foolish at worst. Preachers cannot control the reception of their sermons, but they can pray fervently for the Spirit to enable the reception that agrees with God's will for the listeners' lives and for the health of the congregation.[11]

Unfortunately, there are people in every congregation who intentionally resist the gospel and actively work against it. Ministers should enthusiastically preach to such persons but not forcibly attempt to change them. Certain cases of spiritual transformation require special divine initiative. Once preachers have done their part they should simply move out of the way to make room for God's special intervention in the lives of excessively stubborn persons.

Also, there are many earnest persons in our congregations who eagerly want to receive and be transformed by the gospel. But the anxieties in their lives and even the distractions in the worship service render them susceptible to a distorted or incomplete reception of the gospel in that moment. As C. S. Lewis demonstrated so imaginatively, anxieties and distractions can be chief weapons of the demonic.[12] As the gospel is proclaimed preachers and parishioners need to pray explicitly for the Spirit to minimize the distorting effects of anxieties and distractions. We should also pray for the Spirit to maximize people's concentration and understanding.

As a pastor, I regularly walked through the church sanctuary while it was empty during the week and prayed for good "acoustics" in the upcoming Sunday worship services. The church's financial investment in electronic acoustics would have been in vain without a faith investment in *spiritual* acoustics. Passing by empty pews and imagining the many faces that would soon sit upon them, I asked God to facilitate the reception of my sermons that God intended. Then, on Sundays, before the sermon, I often prayed to myself: "Lord, help me *say* it right. Help them *hear* it right. Help us *live* it right."

Also, I have pastoral colleagues who have enlisted groups of parishioners whose primary ministry is to pray for the pastor and congregation before and during worship services. These persons gather in a room apart from the sanctuary and fervently invite God to pervade the worship service and to empower the redemptive dialogue between pastor and people during the sermon.

The awareness that this kind of intercessory prayer is occurring surely emboldens these pastors and elevates the spiritual awareness of these congregations. Also, in the struggle against evil principalities and powers, prayers for an anointed reception of God's word are an especially effective strategy. Demonic distractions are less likely to deceive people who are alertly focused on God's word as it emerges in worship.

Conclusion

Paul considered himself a specially commissioned messenger of the gospel. Although he offered no extended reflection on preaching, his letters reveal that preaching was the priority in his ministry. In our quest to prioritize preaching, contemporary ministers should consult Paul's ancient wisdom. The consultation might refine our perspectives about why we preach and provide access to new power for that preaching.

Having explored Paul as a messenger of the gospel, we will focus in the next two chapters on how to interpret Paul's Letters as a medium for the gospel. The question, "Why do we preach?" will give way to the question, "How do we preach?"

CHAPTER FOUR

PREACHING PAUL: INTERPRETING PAUL'S LETTERS FOR PROCLAMATION

> *The earliest Christians, including Paul, recognized that*
> *"new occasions teach new duties."... When one talks*
> *about the "traditions" in the early church, one should not*
> *picture sets of theological and ethical teachings tied up in*
> *neat packages, handed on from generation to generation*
> *with the warning, "Do not disturb."... For all of his*
> *respect for traditions, including the ethical ones, Paul, for*
> *example, never confused those traditions, even those*
> *compiled into "scripture," with the gospel, the Word of*
> *God itself.*[1]

I n previous chapters, we have explored *what* preaching is, discussed *who* Paul was, and consulted Paul's Letters for insights
on *why* we preach. The next two chapters impart practical
suggestions concerning *how* to preach from Paul's Letters. In particular, this chapter addresses a primary and essential aspect of
effective preaching: responsible biblical interpretation.

Preaching—the faithful, passionate reporting of God's useful
news—is more than the mere recitation of ancient scripture.
Preaching seeks to pronounce how God's actions, to which scripture testifies, are being fulfilled in the contemporary world.
Nevertheless, it is impossible for preachers to tell the contemporary
gospel story apart from the ancient story narrated in scripture.

Like a wise elder, scripture possesses significant history of and sage counsel about God's encounters with our spiritual ancestors. Only a foolish preacher would set out on any sermonic journey without conversing with that wise elder. This chapter offers instructions for maximizing that conversation.

No sermon, however powerful and polished, is ever the last word on God or a biblical text. Generally a preacher has twenty minutes in a sermon to wrestle with a sacred text that has more than twenty centuries of history. In the face of those odds, wise preachers relinquish fantasies about offering exhaustive biblical interpretations. Instead, such preachers are content to provide faithful interpretations—readings that engage scripture with spiritual imagination and intellectual honesty.

Therefore, my approach to biblical interpretation makes no effort to be comprehensive. Just as more could be said about any biblical passage, more could also be said (and has been said) about approaches to biblical interpretation.[2] At its best biblical interpretation for preaching is a conversation among God, interpreters, and texts. Thus my approach is designed to aid the conversation, ensure that the conversation remains charitable, and foster conditions for the conversation to transform us. Additionally, my forthcoming suggestions bear in mind the time constraints under which most ministers, and especially pastors, labor.

An honest assessment of one's assumptions is a vital aspect of responsible interpretation. First, I will explore more fully my assumptions concerning preaching and the Bible, to which I alluded in chapter 3. Then I will offer a homiletical approach to interpreting Pauline texts, along with examples of the approach.

Preaching and the Bible

When interpreting Pauline passages (or any scripture) in a sermon, a preacher must maintain the proper relationship between the biblical past and the biblical present. The biblical past includes the ancient historical circumstances surrounding the composition and initial reception of scripture. Questions such as, "Who wrote the text?" and "How did ancient communities understand the text?" are always appropriate. These questions remind modern-day interpreters that we are not the first or most perceptive persons ever to grapple with God. A probing investigation of the struggle of our spiritual ancestors can greatly enrich our preaching.

But infatuation with ancient struggles can obscure the primary focus of preaching—the unleashing of God's liberating word in today's communities of faith. Effective preachers remember that "people are really interested in the question *does* God save? rather than in the question *did* God save long ago?"[3] Accordingly, people expect sermons to reveal the biblical present—the unique ways that God's judgment and grace alluded to in scripture manifest themselves in the current moment.

While faithfully remembering the past recorded in scripture, a preacher and a worshiping community affirm that scripture has a present tense. What matters most "is not what lies behind the text in the form of an original meaning but what lies in front of it where the interpreter stands."[4] Thus the very act of preaching boldly testifies that "revelation is never something over and done with or gone for good or in danger of slipping away into the past; it is ongoing."[5] An image might further clarify the relationship between the past and the present in biblical interpretation for preaching.

By considering the relationship of a car's front windshield to its rearview and sideview mirrors, we can see more clearly how the past and present connect in preaching. Proportionately, the front windshield of a car is many times larger than the rearview and sideview mirrors. The size of the front windshield suggests the forward orientation of the driving process. When driving, we need as wide a viewing area as possible to see where we are headed.

Yet before placing a car in gear, a careful driver will glance into the rearview and sideview mirrors. These mirrors are much smaller compared to the front windshield. On the trip, these mirrors are never meant to be the primary focal point. Still, by glancing at objects behind and beside the car many driving disasters can be avoided.

For preachers to be overly concerned about ancient biblical meaning would be the equivalent of driving while staring constantly in the rearview and sideview mirrors. This perpetual backward glance would impede and endanger the community's forward progress into God's present and future. However, preachers who never concern themselves with ancient biblical meaning are an accident waiting to happen. Their failure to gain perspective on where they are by looking at whence they have come is equally reckless.

An analysis of his letters reveals that Paul, too, was passionately invested in the present meaning of biblical texts. In this regard, ministers who preach from Paul's Letters might imitate Paul's interpretive practices. According to Nancy Lammers Gross, preachers should do what Paul does and not simply repeat what Paul says.[6] What does Paul do with scripture?

When interpreting Israel's scripture in light of his Christ encounter, Paul endeavors to find the present word for his community in the ancient text. For Paul the scripture is not a collection of inert doctrines but a dynamic invitation to creative rereading. Paul would have failed his exegetical courses in many contemporary divinity schools. When he cites the Bible he is rarely concerned to ascertain the "historical" meaning of the texts for his religious ancestors. The Bible, for Paul, is a springboard that can propel him to a more flexible and contemporary meaning.

An intriguing example of Paul's interpretive creativity occurs in his reading of the Genesis narrative of Sarah and Hagar in Galatians 4:21-31. One quickly detects his creative liberties with Genesis. In his *contemporary moment* Paul takes the *ancient* biblical text (Genesis) seriously by reading it in fresh and unpredictable ways. He does not abandon the ancient text, nor does he assume that the ancient meaning of the text exhausts its interpretive possibilities.[7]

Paul's contemporary theology was as determinative, if not more so, of meaning as were the historical intentions of the authors who composed the biblical texts. To some extent, Paul was an ancient "reader-response" interpreter. He understood that biblical meaning was created in the conversation between the Bible and the experiences of the reader. Meaning was not a pre-determined changeless message simply waiting to be discovered in the Bible.

As the epigraph beginning this chapter implies, Paul found no "do not disturb" sign on scripture. His letters reflect his "sanctified tampering" with the sacred ancestral tradition. He trespassed on the holy ground of scripture, searching for new revelations from a Holy God. Now that Paul's Letters themselves are part of *our* sacred ancestral tradition, let us find the courage to engage in our own sanctified tampering with the text. The risks of such interpretive trespassing are great, but so are the rewards!

Selecting a Pauline Text for Preaching

When preaching from a Pauline passage (or any biblical text), ministers should be careful to select a manageable amount of scripture. Frequently this means no more than a portion of a chapter, and in my preaching from Paul's Letters I have often focused on one verse in a chapter.

Concerning manageable amounts of scripture, I recall the wisdom of my father, a pastor and pulpit veteran. He once told me, "Son, the gospel is a story with a two-thousand-year history. Don't try to tell it all at once!" His counsel reminds me of the difference between a satisfyingly full sermon and one that lacks focus because it is bloated with too much information and too many objectives. To avoid preaching bloated sermons ministers should select wisely how much text to cover. There are at least four approaches to selecting Pauline texts for preaching.

First, a lectionary—a predetermined three-year cycle of scripture readings—can provide helpful parameters for selecting Pauline passages. For example, both the Roman Catholic Lectionary and the Revised Common Lectionary offer healthy dosages of Pauline texts. The lectionary alleviates the stress of deciding which biblical texts to preach.

But lectionary preachers desiring to proclaim from Pauline texts should occasionally expand beyond the boundaries of the lectionary. For instance, the Revised Common Lectionary omits Galatians 2:1-10. This passage recounts the early church's struggle concerning social diversity between Jews and Gentiles, as well as Paul's commitment to provide financial assistance to impoverished Christians in other parts of the world.

Preachers who never wrestle with this passage miss a grand opportunity to explore the church's ongoing struggle with social diversity. Twenty centuries after Paul there remain significant social barriers separating those of us who are in Christ. Far too often we sing the great hymn of unity "In Christ There Is No East or West" in churches that have mistaken social uniformity for genuine unity. Galatians 2:1-10 could encourage a congregation to acknowledge that the embrace of diversity is essential to Christian unity. Also, this passage could sensitize a congregation to its global responsibility to provide economic assistance to persons in need. Such a message has profound implications in a world where warfare and disease are decimating families, communities, and entire nations.

Second, many preachers—including me—do not follow the lectionary. Generally my personal reading of scripture and the needs and concerns of the congregation influence my selection of texts for preaching. Also, my selection is based on adherence to major moments in the liturgical year, such as Advent, Christmas, Lent, Easter, and Pentecost. Additionally, I take into account worship traditions and celebrations specific to the congregation. By considering these and other factors, nonlectionary preachers can expose congregations to the diversity of scripture and not subject congregations simply to the preacher's favorite passages. Let me illustrate in various ways how the above influences have guided my selection of Pauline texts.

Once during my pastorate I preached a five-part sermon series entitled "Christianity 101." Exploring foundational aspects of Christian belief and practice, the sermons addressed issues such as God's character and the salvation that God offers through Christ. Since Paul was one of the first practical theologians in the church, and since his letters are historically the earliest texts in the New Testament, I decided to lean heavily on Pauline passages for that series.

In a series on Christian basics, I felt that at least one sermon had to examine the practice of the Lord's Supper. I planned the series so that this particular sermon would occur on the first Sunday of the month, which was the monthly celebration of the Lord's Supper in that congregation.

Knowing that Paul discusses the Lord's Supper in 1 Corinthians 11:17-34, I preached a sermon from that passage entitled "Table Talk." The sermon focused on the assertion in verse 26 that the Lord's Supper itself is a sermon. The communion table, which holds the elements of the Lord's Supper, proclaims to us Christ's past suffering and our future salvation. Thus, my familiarity with Pauline texts converged with the congregation's need for ongoing instruction in Christian basics, as well as with the congregation's worship traditions around the Lord's Supper.

On another occasion in my pastorate, the congregation was engaged in an extensive renovation of the church's facilities. As I talked with the construction contractors they ensured me that the work, though incomplete, would soon be finished. Immediately their observations called to mind that great Pauline affirmation in Philippians 1:6: "I am confident of this, that [God] who began a good work among you will bring it to completion by the day of Jesus Christ." The following Sunday I preached a sermon from that text entitled "Under Construction." Since each believer's spiritual development is a work in progress, the sermon declared that an "under construction" sign could be placed on each person. Yet in spite of the perpetual demolition and renovation in our spiritual lives, we could all rest assured that God would complete the work. In this instance, an event in the life of the congregation unrelated to the liturgical year—a church renovation—prompted the selection of a Pauline text.

A third approach to selecting Pauline texts is *lectio continua*, which is Latin for "continuous reading." This is a process of reading and preaching through an entire Pauline Letter or a section of one. Several of Paul's Letters are short enough to enable a minister to cover significant portions of the letter in a brief sermon series.

I rarely, if ever, preach a sermon series longer than eight weeks. I have discovered that after eight weeks both the congregation and I begin to grow weary of a text or topic, regardless of its importance. Thus, unless ministers are extremely captivating orators, they should probably not preach continuously through Romans or 1 Corinthians. A preacher, however, could base a series of sermons on large sections of a Pauline Letter on an annual basis. For example, one year a minister might preach a series on Romans 1–3 and the next year on 1 Corinthians 1–4.

A fourth approach is *lectio selecta*, which is Latin for "selected reading." This involves choosing passages on a thematic basis rather than the continuous reading in order from week to week. A minister could offer a sermon series examining Paul's treatment of the Holy Spirit, the church, or even the handling of communal conflict in various letters. Or, one could examine a theme as it emerges in one letter. For instance, my colleague Diane Wudel recently conducted a teaching series in a church where she examined issues of bodies in 1 Corinthians—physical bodies, the church as a body, and the resurrected body of Christ.

Preachers adopting a thematic approach to text selection should avoid harmonizing the thematic differences that emerge in Paul's Letters. For instance, Paul's approach to community conflict in one letter may differ from that in another letter. By allowing those differences to surface in sermons, preachers expose the influence of context and circumstance on theology, whether ancient or modern. Whatever approach is used, text selection is a crucial aspect of the interpretive process and deserves critical reflection.

An Interpretive Approach

Once a Pauline text is selected, the following interpretive suggestions can enable a responsible, creative handling of that text in the pulpit. These suggestions make no claims to originality. My approach is a mixture of my practices and the best insights from colleagues.

Effective biblical interpretation for preaching requires multiple readings of a biblical text. Like traveling in a circle, the interpreter seemingly covers the same textual ground, but in actuality each trip around the circle represents forward progress.[8] The wisdom from and about a text during one trip around the circle transforms earlier insights and is transformed by those earlier insights. Thus, a curved—not straight—line connects these recommendations.

In an effort to show and not simply tell, I offer examples of this approach using Romans 8:26-30. In the next chapter I will present a sermon that I have preached on this text. By presenting my interpretive process with Romans 8 in this chapter along with a sermon on this text in the next chapter, I demonstrate the integral connection between interpretation and sermon creation.[9]

I have placed suggested time limits in parentheses for each step of the journey. Obviously, there is an arbitrary quality to these time limits. The time needed for each step is dependent on multiple factors such as one's overall familiarity with Pauline texts, the nature and difficulty of the selected text, and one's access to and expertise with various critical tools such as commentaries. Also, the suggested limits do not include the additional time needed for composing the sermon manuscript with its introduction, images, and conclusion. I usually devote another eight to ten hours beyond the interpretive phase, creating, polishing, and rehearsing a sermon manuscript.

The recommended time limits for the interpretive phase convey two worthwhile lessons. First, a disciplined approach to interpretation is actually a time-saving technique. Several intense but brief engagements with a passage spread over a few days can yield a great interpretive harvest, while also freeing up time for other familial and professional commitments.

Second, the recommended time frames should also caution ministers about the dangers of interpretive haste. Regardless of a minister's professional expertise and experience, sermons served up too quickly rarely have much "nutritional value." To be sure, not every sermonic meal demands the elaborate preparation given to a holiday dinner. Still, parishioners with discriminating palates can easily distinguish between fast food and home cooking.

Initial Impressions of a Text (fifteen minutes)

Too often preachers rush to the commentaries and other critical scholarship before solidifying their own perceptions about a text. Thus, I encourage preachers to form their own imaginative impressions of a text through the following strategies:

- First, invite the Holy Spirit into the interpretive process.

- Second, read the selected passage aloud several times, or have it read to you. By making oral readings of the text a regular part of their early interpretations, preachers "reoralize" written texts—an important reminder that these written texts were also intended to be read.[10] For instance, Paul's Letters were read aloud in his congregations.

- Third, make a list of "images" in the text. In this initial stage preachers should unshackle their imaginations and jot down anything that arrests their attention, most especially the sensory features in the text. The list need not be organized or lengthy. It can be created in "bullet-point" fashion.

Preachers might also consider how other people may react initially to this passage. So, two questions can be asked: What grips me, and what potentially might grip particular persons in my congregation? The consideration of other people's reactions reminds preachers that they are never solo interpreters. Preachers interpret in and for a community. Also, promising material for sermon introductions, images, and conclusions emerge in the process of imaging the text.[11]

Initial Impressions of Romans 8:26-30: An Example

²⁶Likewise the Spirit helps us in our weakness; for we do not know how to pray as we ought, but that very Spirit intercedes with sighs too deep for words. ²⁷And God, who searches the heart, knows what is the mind of the Spirit, because the Spirit intercedes for the saints according to the will of God. ²⁸We know that all things work together for good for those who love God, who are called according to his purpose. ²⁹For those whom he foreknew he also predestined to be conformed to the image of his Son, in order that he might be the firstborn within a large family. ³⁰And those whom he predestined he also called; and those whom he called he also justified; and those whom he justified he also glorified.

After reading this passage aloud several times, my list of initial impressions contained the following:

- Human weakness

- How does the Spirit help?

- Blockages to our prayer lives

- Human ignorance and inability

- Sighs that cannot be expressed in words

- God and the Spirit are close and connected.

- Verse 26 brings me hope.

- The end of the passage is repetitive; sounds lyrical, even musical; closes on a victorious note.

- Family language is used: "son" and "firstborn."

- What weaknesses exist in the life of the congregation?

Notice that the list contains fragments of sentences and thoughts, as well as questions. Also, the list does not completely follow the order of the text. The goal here is simply to place oneself in the orbit of the text, allowing the text's gravitational pull to draw one closer.

A Close Reading of a Text (six hours)

Next, preachers need to refine and revise their initial impressions of and preliminary questions about a text. A series of close readings of a text can aid this process. Imagination is needed as much in this phase as it was in the earlier phase.

But in our close readings of a text we yoke our imagination to a set of disciplined procedures and allow the two driving forces of responsible interpretation—imagination and discipline—to advance our interpretive journey. While mindful that interpretation is rarely this neat or orderly, I nevertheless have divided the close reading phase into three parts for clarity of instruction: literary analysis, historical and rhetorical analysis, and theological and contextual analysis. A minister might allow approximately two hours of preparation for each kind of analysis.

Also, it can be helpful to separate each phase of analysis by a short span of time. For example, after an hour of intense work with a text, a minister might take a short walk, have a cup of tea, or return phone calls and e-mails. These breaks restore focus and replenish energy.

Literary Analysis (two hours)

By literary analysis I mean detailed investigation of the language of a passage, including its words, idioms, and overall context. The following four steps might enable a solid literary analysis:

- *First, investigate carefully the English translation (or prepare a translation if you have ability with the ancient languages*). Just like middle-school students diagramming sentences in English class, ministers should pay attention to the nouns, verbs, commands, and descriptive phrases in every sentence. Unknown, unusual, or repeated words, phrases, and themes should be flagged for further investigation.

- *Second, examine unknown, unusual, or repeated words, phrases, and themes using resources such as biblical or theological dictionaries.*

- *Third, establish the larger literary context for the passage.* Ministers should always read their selected text in light of passages that precede and follow it. Also, knowledge of the overarching themes and concerns of the biblical book one is reading can be very helpful. The introductions in study Bibles and commentaries, as well as introductory textbooks to the Old and New Testaments, can greatly assist with such overviews. Ministers might note if words, phrases, or themes in the selected passage appear in the wider literary context. A concordance is an excellent tool for this kind of examination.

- *Fourth, review the list of initial impressions in light of the literary analysis.*

Literary Analysis of Romans 8:26-30: An Example

In this example, I work with the English translation, although I refer to elements of the Greek that can be easily obtained in dictionaries and commentaries.

> ²⁶Likewise the Spirit helps us in our weakness; for we do not know how to pray as we ought, but that very Spirit intercedes with sighs too deep for words. ²⁷And God, who searches the

heart, knows what is the mind of the Spirit, because the Spirit intercedes for the saints according to the will of God. [28]We know that all things work together for good for those who love God, who are called according to his purpose. [29]For those whom he foreknew he also predestined to be conformed to the image of his Son, in order that he might be the firstborn within a large family. [30]And those whom he predestined he also called; and those whom he called he also justified; and those whom he justified he also glorified.

- The word *Spirit* occurs four times in this passage. On three occasions the word *Spirit* is the subject of verbs: "the Spirit helps" (v. 26); "the Spirit intercedes" (v. 26); and "the Spirit intercedes" (v. 27).

- The word *we* occurs three times in this passage: "we do not know" (v. 26); "we ought" (v. 26); and "we know" (v. 28).

- The word *God* occurs explicitly three times in this passage. Once, *God* is the subject of a verb: "God knows" (v. 27). Twice, *God* is used objectively: "the will of God" (v. 27) and "those who love God" (v. 28). Also, God is referred to several times with the pronouns *his* and *he* (vv. 28-30).

- Given the prevalence of the Spirit in the passage, I should explore more fully the word *Spirit*. A Bible dictionary quickly reveals that the Greek New Testament word for *Spirit* is also the word for *wind* (*pneuma*).

- According to commentaries, the Greek verb translated "to help" in verse 26 means "to join with to help" or "to lend a hand." This observation, coupled with the double meaning of *pneuma*, has rich homiletical potential. Thus, another translation of verse 26 could be: "Likewise, the wind lends us a hand in our weakness."

- Examining verses 26-30 in the context of the rest of Romans 8, I discover that there are numerous references to the Holy Spirit (for example, vv. 1-16), as well as to human weakness and suffering (for example, vv. 18-25 and vv. 35-38). In spite of the weakness and suffering, the passage ends on a resounding note of victory (vv. 35-39).

- Now I understand better the hope of verse 26 that I sensed in my initial readings. The hope is based on the Spirit "giving us a hand" in our weakness.

This example demonstrates that literary analysis can be detailed without being lengthy or overly technical. I investigated some basic literary features on my own before turning to resource materials. Also, notice how the literary analysis is already creating homiletical focus.

There are many important details in verses 27-30 that could be considered, but the earlier portion of verse 26 has especially captivated my attention and imagination. Whereas it would be unwise to ignore totally other details in verses 27-30, I might concentrate on verse 26. Clearly, Romans 8:26-30 contains interpretive data for many sermons. Thus, I recall my dad's advice: "The gospel is a story with a two-thousand-year history. Don't try to tell it all at once!"

Historical and Rhetorical Analysis (two hours)

Preachers can employ basic historical and rhetorical approaches in pragmatic ways to enrich their understanding of scripture. My brief comments about historical analysis will be followed by even more concise observations about rhetorical analysis.

Historical analysis involves investigation of the circumstances surrounding the composition and reception of a text by its initial author and audiences. This kind of interpretation requires not only historical data but also historical imagination to envision the larger social world in which a text emerged.

For example, an important (and assumed) feature of Paul's world is the Roman Empire. As demonstrated in chapter 2, Paul occasionally challenges Roman imperial culture by offering Christian reinterpretations of terms used by imperial culture. Thus attention to social, economic, and political factors in the ancient world can provide preachers with profound perspectives on scripture. Already in our literary analysis above we explored some historical concerns when we investigated the double meaning of the word *pneuma*. This overlap between literary and historical analysis reminds us not to establish rigid boundaries between the proposed interpretive categories.

Important tools for historical study include biblical commentaries and introductory textbooks to the Old and New Testaments. Also, I highly recommend that preachers add to their libraries Everett Ferguson's *Backgrounds of Early Christianity*, 3d edition (Grand Rapids: William B. Eerdmans, 2003). This book provides accessible, essential information about the important groups, historical practices, and cultural attitudes surrounding the emergence of early Christianity.

Furthermore, an often neglected historical feature of a text is the history of its interpretation. An examination of how others have grappled with Pauline texts across Christian history can impart much homiletical wisdom. Some biblical commentaries provide observations about a text's interpretive history. Additionally, preachers might want to consult and even buy the *Ancient Christian Commentary on Scripture*, vols. 6-9 (Downers Grove, Ill.: InterVarsity Press, 1998–2000). This commentary's volumes on the Pauline Letters present the interpretations of early church leaders such as Origen and Augustine. One can also locate the history of interpretation in other creative media such as plays, artwork, and movies. For instance, Robert Jewett has chronicled the many ways that Pauline texts and themes have appeared in cinema (*Saint Paul at the Movies: The Apostle's Dialogue with American Culture* [Louisville: Westminster John Knox Press, 1993]).

Whereas preachers should familiarize themselves with ancient historical details of a text, I renew my admonition to avoid a preoccupation with ancient history in the pulpit. Without some restraint, a sermon can easily become an exposition of ancient history rather than a proclamation of a contemporary word.

Certainly, at times, ancient historical details are crucial for sermons. For instance, earlier I mentioned the value of preaching a sermon from Galatians 2:1-10. Such a sermon would require a brief historical investigation of the social diversity in Paul's congregations. On other occasions, ancient details serve only as joists. In architecture, joists are large beams supporting a floor or ceiling. While not seen, joists are still present and necessary. Similarly, substantive historical work should support our preaching, although it might never be heard directly in a sermon. Now let me offer a concise word about rhetorical analysis.

As the art of persuasion, rhetoric explores how a person communicates a message to an audience. More specifically, rhetorical analysis investigates a speaker's argument and the actions the speaker desires the audience to take. In a rhetorical analysis, a preacher might ask the following questions: In Paul's arguments in this passage, does he try to convince on the basis of scripture, his authority as an apostle, a common experience he shared with a congregation, emotional appeal, or other factors? What action(s) does Paul expect his audience to take as a result of his words?

In short, historical and rhetorical analysis investigates the author, audience, argument, and action. (Of course, a book on preaching would be incomplete without some alliteration.)

The following five steps might enable a solid historical and rhetorical analysis:

- *First, explore details concerning the author.* Whereas we know that Paul is the author of these letters, we should ask questions about his geographical location when writing and his stated reasons for writing.

- *Second, explore details concerning the audience.* Each of the recipients of Paul's Letters—whether entire congregations or specific individuals—possessed distinguishing characteristics that might enliven a preacher's imagination. An exploration of the author and audience in Pauline texts will often necessitate familiarity with cultural institutions and practices referred to in the text. For example, insights on Greco-Roman sporting events can enable deeper understanding of the athletic images Paul uses. I encourage preachers to buy David J. Williams's *Paul's Metaphors: Their Context and Character* (Peabody, Mass.: Hendrickson Publishers, 1999). This book provides concise illustrative insights about the institutions and practices that influenced Paul's life, letters, and congregations.

- *Third, assess Paul's argument in the text.*

- *Fourth, determine the action the text intends for its audience.*

- *Fifth, review the list of initial impressions in light of the historical and rhetorical analysis.*

Historical and Rhetorical Analysis of Romans 8:26-30: An Example

[26]Likewise the Spirit helps us in our weakness; for we do not know how to pray as we ought, but that very Spirit intercedes with sighs too deep for words. [27]And God, who searches the heart, knows what is the mind of the Spirit, because the Spirit intercedes for the saints according to the will of God. [28]We know that all things work together for good for those who love God, who are called according to his purpose. [29]For those whom he foreknew he also predestined to be conformed to the image of his Son, in order that he might be the firstborn within a large family. [30]And those whom he predestined he also called; and those whom he called he also justified; and those whom he justified he also glorified.

- Author: The commentaries reveal that Paul wrote the Letter to the Romans from Corinth late in his ministry. Unlike many other congregations to which he wrote, he did not found the Roman congregation. So his relationship with this church is very different. Some scholars say that Paul wrote this letter to prepare for a future trip to Rome.

- Audience: There is much debate in the commentaries about the identity of the Roman congregation. Scholars do not agree on whether the congregation was composed predominantly of Jews or Gentiles, or whether it contained a substantial mixture of both. Given certain statements in other parts of the letter (for example, Rom. 11 and 14), we might assume that there has been turmoil in the congregation. My initial assessment is that issues concerning the author and the audience do not directly affect the message of Romans 8:26-30. The message of that text in some ways stands independent of these historical concerns.

- Argument: The word *likewise* at the beginning of verse 26 seems important. It apparently connects what Paul is about to say to what he has just said. In verses 18-25, Paul discusses the suffering that comes from living in a world riddled with sin and decay. He also mentions the forthcoming glory that believers will enjoy. Perhaps the Spirit is the power source that enables believers to endure the suffering as they await the glory.

- Action: Paul's goal in verses 26-30 seems to be encouragement and motivation.

- My historical and rhetorical analysis continues to support my initial interest in verse 26 and the role of the Spirit in the midst of human weakness.

Theological and Contextual Analysis (two hours)

Theological analysis explores a text's perspective on God's nature, God's relationship with the entire creation, and our relationships with the entire creation in light of God. Contextual analysis explores the impact of people's social identities on their perceptions of texts and of the world. Briefly, I will define the contributions of each analysis.

Theological analysis serves two important purposes in preaching. First, it ensures that our preaching maintains an appropriate focus on God. So much preaching misses the mark because it fails to keep the main thing the main thing, which is God's righteous intentions for the world, loving involvement with the world, and future reign over the world. While positively influencing the creation and its inhabitants, the gospel begins and ends with God. Preaching is not the stringing together of funny, riveting, or even religious *human-interest* stories; it is the proclamation of *God's* story.

Second, theological analysis enables preachers to refine their understandings of God, lest those understandings become restrictive. Preachers can slip into theological ruts and depict God in their sermons in utterly predictable and stagnant ways. Whereas it is appropriate for preachers to have a set of foundational depictions of God, we must remember how vast and diverse are scripture's images of God. These different and sometimes competing images "shake us free from more defined symbols to an awareness of the immensity of God."[12]

It is difficult for our hearers to appreciate the immensity of God if preachers always drag God into their theological ruts. Or, to appropriate an image from one of my students, many sermons "hamstring" God. Instead of allowing the elusive mysterious God to run freely across people's imaginations, worn out sermonic images sever God's mobility. Theological analysis restores mobility to God, inviting God to transport preachers and listeners into uncharted territories.

Preachers can pose a variety of questions to a text to investigate its theological aspects.[13] I have organized some potential questions under the following six headings: *creation* (Where did we come from?); *covenant* (How does God deal with us?); *sin* (How do we mess up the relationship?); *redemption* (How does God clean up our mess?); *community* (How do we live Christ-shaped lives with one another?); and *destiny* (Where are we going from here?). Frequently, one or more of the above theological concerns are central in a text.

Contextual analysis reminds us that interpreters are never neutral. People are always trying to satisfy needs and pursue interests based on their social contexts and personal identities. The quest to meet needs or pursue interests can create harmony and cooperation among people, or disagreement and even strife. Consequently, human existence is political and involves constant, complex negotiations of power as people fulfill their needs.

Contextual analysis examines the impact of people's social contexts and personal identities upon the pursuit of their needs. This examination prevents preachers from becoming naive about the power dynamics in scripture and in their interpretations of scripture. Preachers should raise questions about the social contexts in scripture, as well as the social contexts in which their interpretations of scripture occur.

For example, an interpretation of 1 Corinthians might be much richer if preachers kept in mind issues of gender and social class in the ancient world. Preachers might ask this question: To what degree are Paul's comments in 1 Corinthians affected by his male gender and by the apparently high economic status of certain Corinthian converts? Obviously, the answers to these questions involve some speculation, but the speculation might open new vistas on our interpretations.

Also, preachers should interpret their own social contexts, assessing the impact of their personal identities on their interpretations. These identities would include, but not be limited to, their family relationships, institutional memberships, cultural assumptions, ethnicity, gender, class status, sexual orientation, nationality, and religious heritage, to name a few.

Preachers might ask this question: What is it about my identity that draws me to certain features in a text while causing me
to ignore others? The inclusion of these contemporary social factors does not compromise our interpretations. On the contrary,
the failure to include such concerns is what potentially compro-
mises the message of scripture and the truth of the gospel.[14]

The following four steps might enable a solid theological and
contextual analysis:

- *First, pose explicitly theological questions to a text.*
  Ministers might use categories such as creation,
  covenant, sin, redemption, community, and destiny.

- *Second, raise questions about the social contexts in
  scripture.* Examine where issues concerning the use
  and distribution of power emerge. Do these power
  issues create cooperation or conflict in the text?

- *Third, raise questions about your own social contexts.*

- *Fourth, refine your initial impressions of a text based on
  the theological and contextual analysis.*

Theological and Contextual Analysis of Romans 8:26-30: An Example

26Likewise the Spirit helps us in our weakness; for we do not
know how to pray as we ought, but that very Spirit intercedes
with sighs too deep for words. 27And God, who searches the
heart, knows what is the mind of the Spirit, because the Spirit
intercedes for the saints according to the will of God. 28We
know that all things work together for good for those who love
God, who are called according to his purpose. 29For those
whom he foreknew he also predestined to be conformed to the
image of his Son, in order that he might be the firstborn within
a large family. 30And those whom he predestined he also called;

and those whom he called he also justified; and those whom he justified he also glorified.

- Theological analysis: Whereas the passage explores several theological issues, two appear prominent: "covenant" and "destiny." God relates to us through God's Spirit, who assists us in our weaknesses. That covenant relationship will ultimately ensure believers' destiny with God. We will be justified by God and glorified with God at the end (v. 30).

- Social context in the text: In some sense, issues of "power" are not prominent in this text. Paul suggests that humans are often powerless and thus must depend on God.

- Social context of the interpreter: My African American Christian heritage has greatly stressed the role of the Holy Spirit. Thus I am comfortable with Paul's emphasis on the Spirit. The language of weakness in this passage is a helpful challenge to my "male ego" as well. Many men are uncomfortable admitting their weaknesses. Also, as a man striving to be more gender inclusive, I am struck by Paul's use of male imagery to depict God and Jesus. God is consistently referred to as "he." Christ is called "Son."

- The theological and contextual analysis continues to support my initial impressions of this passage.

From the Good Book to the Good News

As suggested in chapter 3, the above interpretive procedures, though crucial, are not an end unto themselves. Rigorous academic investigation of a text is simply preparation for deeper communion with God that can occur in the devotional interpretation of a text. Having gained familiarity with various aspects of a text through the outlined procedures, a preacher should ask prayerfully: What must my congregation and I do in response to this scripture?

This question ensures that sermons become more than simple recitations of scripture. Colloquially, many people refer to the Bible as the "Good Book."[15] As important as the Good Book is in preaching, our ultimate responsibility is to proclaim the *good news*. The Good Book and the good news are related, but they are not necessarily identical. Thus, interpretive procedures might reveal what a text says, but intense prayer is also needed to discern what God is saying to a congregation through a text.

As preachers move forward in their sermon creation they should identify the sermon's main message and objective. Homileticians use a wide variety of terms for this process. For example, Thomas Long refers to a sermon's *focus* ("what the sermon aims to say") and its *function* ("what the sermon aims to do").[16] Henry Mitchell speaks of the *controlling idea* (the primary message emerging from scripture) and the *behavioral purpose* of a sermon (the sermon's desired effect upon hearers' behavior).[17] With my students I use the terminology of *gospel claim* (What is the good news in this sermon?) and *gospel conduct* (What does this good news call us to do?).

If a preacher rigorously explores and fervently meditates over scripture, much of a sermon's content will be readily present. When a preacher identifies a clear gospel claim and gospel conduct, "a sermon will almost write itself."[18]

From my work with Romans 8:26-30, the gospel claim has emerged: the Spirit/wind lends us a hand in our weakness. Likewise, the gospel conduct based on that claim is: perseverance (Hold on in spite of the weakness!). In a reasonable amount of time (approximately six hours), my interpretive efforts have yielded a workable sermonic approach to this text. This leaves me ample time to compose a sermon manuscript filled with poignant prose and gripping images.

Conclusion

Responsible biblical interpretation is a vital aspect of effective preaching. With the Spirit's guidance a preacher's imaginative and disciplined engagements with scripture can provide a wealth of questions, insights, and images from which a compelling message can emerge. In the next chapter, I will demonstrate how my interpretation of Romans 8:26-30 gave rise to a sermon on that passage. After presenting the sermon manuscript, I will explore certain theological and rhetorical features of this sermon to illustrate how theology and rhetoric can assist our preaching from Paul's Letters.

CHAPTER FIVE

PREACHING PAUL: PROCLAIMING THE NEWS FROM PAUL'S LETTERS

> *The good news about Jesus should sound more important*
> *than the evening news with Peter Jennings.*[1]

This chapter expands the book's emphasis on preaching method. Specifically, I explore theological and rhetorical considerations of preaching from Paul's Letters. I accomplish this in four ways: (1) I present the manuscript from an actual sermon that I have preached on Romans 8:26-30—the sample text from the last chapter. (2) I analyze certain theological and rhetorical features of this sermon. (3) I provide the manuscripts from two other sermons that I have preached on Pauline texts; and (4) I include critiques of these two sermons by colleagues—a biblical scholar and homiletician and a journalist.

As I suggested in chapter 1, preaching is the faithful passionate reporting of God's useful news. Thus, this book would be imbalanced if I simply talked about reporting the news but never included any of my own "broadcasts."

A Pauline Sermon on Romans 8

Initially, I preached the following sermon at Douglas Memorial Community Church in Baltimore, Maryland, when I was the senior pastor. The occasion was Pentecost Sunday, the annual celebration of the Holy Spirit's ministry in the church. The present version of this sermon is a minor adaptation preached in worship services since 2001. The alterations to the original manuscript involved only a slight tightening of the prose, but no significant modification of the sermon's substance. For all intents and purposes the present manuscript reflects typical pulpit work during my pastorate. I did not have weeks to brood over this message. It was conceived and developed in a week's time.

Before presenting the sermon, two other observations are in order. First, I am an unashamed manuscript preacher. I reject homiletical debates about the superiority or inferiority of manuscript or nonmanuscript preaching. Early in my ministry a cherished personal conversation with Gardner Taylor, a crown prince of the pulpit, solidified my commitment to manuscript preaching. Taylor told me, "If you're going to read [your sermons], read well. My colleague Sandy Ray read nearly every word he preached. But my, what reading it was!"[2]

I tell my students that competent preachers should know how to preach with and without a manuscript, and then they should choose the method that suits their personality and ministry gifts. Given my fascination with language and my approach to sermon creation, manuscripts have greatly aided my preaching ministry.

Second, even as a manuscript preacher I fully recognize that a manuscript is never a sermon. A manuscript is simply the written transcript for an embodied performance.[3] In the preaching moment, God does not speak through the inanimate words embalmed in 12-point font on 8½-x-11 sheets of paper. God speaks as the preacher and congregation enliven the words of a manuscript through the preacher's impassioned delivery and emphatic gestures and the congregation's thoughtful and enthusiastic reception.

This sermon bears the marks of its original setting—an exuberant African American worship service replete with the vocal involvement of the congregation. Nevertheless, I have preached this same sermon in white congregations. The appreciative comments of white congregants have convinced me that the truth of this sermon traveled, irrespective of ethnic and denominational differences.

Second Wind
(Romans 8:26-27)

I am a serious sports fan. Football is my first love. If I had been twelve inches taller, two seconds faster, and one hundred pounds heavier, I would have been the best offensive lineman that college or professional football has ever seen. Lacking the necessary physical attributes for college football, I ended my formal athletic career after high school. Yet I have remained very active in sports. Now my game is racquetball. I love to watch and play sports.

When a good football or basketball game is on television I will change my schedule to watch it. Having been involved in athletics most of my life I know there is a phenomenon that is every athlete's best friend and perhaps greatest asset.

In athletics, sheer natural ability is always a plus. Yet sometimes athletes can compensate for deficiencies in talent by superior training. In athletics, size can be very important, especially in contact sports like football and basketball. However, when Spud Webb, the former NBA guard who is shorter than I am, won the dunking contest several years ago, he showed that size in sports is not everything.

In athletics, desire is an important attribute. Still, no matter how much desire athletes have, if their technique is poor they will frequently be on the losing side. Nevertheless, even excellent athletic technique is no good if an athlete is out of position on the field or court. Ability, size, desire, technique, and position— each of these is important. But an athlete's best friend is this thing called "second wind."

Second wind is an intangible reality, but every winning athlete knows something about it. Second wind—that breath of vitality that comes seemingly from nowhere. Second wind—that additional surge of energy. Second wind—that extra bit of "juice" when you thought you were "juiced out." Second wind—that last little pep in your step when you were too pooped to pop. Second wind—that last bit of jump in the fourth quarter. Second wind— it's hard to describe it, difficult to define it, not easy to explain it apart from experiencing it. But an athlete's best friend is second wind.

Second wind, in short, is that phenomenon in the heat of competition that permits us to rise above our current fatigue and limitations in order to achieve the desired goal. We can have ability, size, desire, technique, and even be in perfect position to score a touchdown or catch the "alley-oop" pass. But if we are fatigued, and there is no second wind about to blow, we are at a serious disadvantage.

I have watched sprints, relay races, and marathons where the deciding factor was second wind. I have seen boxing and tennis matches where the opponents had equal talent. Yet what tipped the scale in one athlete's favor was second wind. Often, the difference between winning and losing is second wind.

You might be a weekend athlete, or you might have never participated in athletics a day in your life. Yet the message I have for you today is that you, too, can experience second wind. Second wind is not just for great athletes like Muhammad Ali, Michael Jordan, Emmett Smith, or Venus and Serena Williams. Every child of God has access to the second wind!

Ever since the church's birthday on the day of Pentecost, second wind has been available for every twice-born child of God. In the New Testament, the Greek word for the Holy Spirit is *pneuma. Pneuma* is also the New Testament word for "wind."

In that classic dialogue between Jesus and Nicodemus in the Gospel of John, Jesus offers a subtle play on words using the double meaning of the word *pneuma.* Jesus says to Nicodemus that the wind blows where it wills. The word for "wind" is also the word for "spirit." So Jesus teaches us that there is something about the Holy Spirit that is analogous to the wind.

The Holy Spirit is perhaps most windlike in that it is accessible to everyone but can be controlled by no one. Members of certain charismatically oriented denominations can have access to the "wind," but no one can control it. No one can pin the Spirit down. The Spirit is often depicted as a wind in the Bible. Today I want to liken the Holy Spirit to the second wind needed in the heat of competition.

In Romans 8, Paul reflects upon the implications of a life lived under the power of the Holy Spirit. In Romans 8:26, Paul declares, "Likewise the Spirit helps us in our weakness."

If you are weak, or in the words of the song, if you are "weary, worn, and sad";[4] if you are wrestling with disappointment and despair; if the cares of finances and family are frustrating you to no end; if the death or sickness of a loved one is snatching the vitality from your life; if there is any weakness in your life; I have some advice for you. Don't give up the fight; don't throw in the towel; keep on running; keep on striding; because you might be on the verge of catching your second wind. Paul says the *pneuma*—the wind—the Holy Spirit helps us in our weakness.

The role of the Holy Spirit in boosting us through and over our weaknesses and obstacles is a vital truth in Romans 8. Before Romans 8 Paul has only alluded to the Holy Spirit a few times in this letter. In Romans 8, however, Paul refers to the Spirit multiple times! Having laid a doctrinal foundation, Paul begins a discourse on power. In effect, Paul says, "I have given you my doctrines of justification and of sin, but now I need to talk to you about power."

Surely, the church needs more power! Doctrine without power is irrelevant. Theology without power is impotent. Ethics without power is moral futility. Liturgy without power is lifeless. The church without power is a social club. Praying without power is a useless monologue. A trustee board meeting without power is organized deadness. A deacon board meeting without power is pious parading. Bible study without power is a weekly book club. Singing without power is sanctimonious noise. Preaching without power is meaningless chatter. If our witness and lives are to truly make a difference for Christ, we need the power of the second wind, which is the Holy Spirit.

Are there some areas in your life where you are weak or fatigued? Physical fatigue is a bad condition, but mental and spiritual fatigue is even worse. When you are tired and weak in your mind and spirit, you are most vulnerable. The enemy loves to attack us when we are tired and weak. Rarely will Satan unleash the most ferocious attacks on us after we have just read our morning devotions, prayed, and have our minds full of positive thoughts and godly aspirations.

The Evil One is not going to get us when we are at the pinnacle of our anointing. Satan wants to attack us when we are weak, and this is precisely why we need the Holy Spirit to play an active role in our lives, because the Spirit is our second wind that helps us overcome our weakness. Thank God for the second wind!

My sole purpose today is to instruct you about the second wind. But of course, if I am talking about a second wind, then logically there must also be a first wind. As I understand it, the first wind is our personal skill and wherewithal. The first wind is human ability, and by no means do I want to disqualify human ability.

Human ability has a place. God has gifted each of us to do many things—and some things with extraordinary skill. Let us not underestimate or discredit human ability. By the same token, let us not deify and idolize our ability either.

The deifying of human ability creates a spiritually debilitating condition called humanism. Humanism is the misplaced belief that humans can handle all of their problems by themselves. Often, middle-class professionals suffer from mild or even acute cases of humanism.

The first wind, which is our God-given ability, plays an important role. I have discovered that in the church there are two large groups of people, each with a faulty understanding of the first wind. Some people rely on their first wind for *everything;* others rely on their first wind for *nothing.*

Some people think that they can handle all their problems with their expertise, intelligence, savvy, know-how, contacts, connections, and hookups. They rely too heavily on the first wind. The second group, however, never uses their first wind— their gifts and intellect. They depend upon God to do for them things that God has equipped them to do for themselves. The first group consists of rugged individualists, and the second group consists of out-of-touch spiritualists. Each group represents a faulty premise.

To use the first wind to the exclusion of the second wind is an invitation to futility. To wait only for the second wind without ever accessing your first wind is a manifestation of irresponsibility. Do not let my focus today on the second wind of the Spirit blind you to the importance of the first wind. In life, we have to do our part. Don't relegate the Holy Spirit to some kind of invisible genie that you can summon by saying the magic words.

The Holy Spirit gets unfairly put-upon by a lot of lazy, unprepared, and undisciplined Christians. The Spirit will never allow us to exploit the Spirit because of our laziness. The Holy Spirit is often blamed for our lack of preparation and commitment, and also for our unwillingness to be patient and prayerful. We have to do our part. This is the first wind. But by the same token, we should not think that we can do it all by ourselves.

This is the message of the text. There comes a time when we can't do it by ourselves. There comes a time in our race when we run out of strength. There comes a time when we have done all that is in our power to do, and still we are unable. Intelligence runs out; contacts and connections fail; professional training becomes bankrupt. That's when, according to Paul, the second wind kicks in. "Likewise," says Paul, "the Spirit helps us in our weakness."

The context of spiritual empowerment is human weakness. The Spirit cannot have the Spirit's way until we admit our weakness. Or, to paraphrase Ralph West, if we can admit that we have a weakness, then we are about to enter miracle territory.[5]

There is an inextricable link between spiritual power and human problems. If you are weak today; if you are tired today; if you are worn out today, then you are a prime candidate for the renewing and refreshing anointing of the Holy Spirit. Your second wind might be just around the corner.

In verse 26, when Paul says we don't know how to pray, he is not questioning our ability to pray. He is suggesting that even when we do pray, we often don't know the right things for which to pray. Here, the New King James Version might be more accurate to the meaning of this verse when it says, "For we do not know what we should pray for as we ought."

Sometimes life will throw us such a curve that we don't even know what to ask God for. Sometimes situations can have us so dazed and crazed that we don't even know where to begin our conversation with God. Have you ever been so befuddled, so confused, so overwhelmed that you did not know how to pray? It is precisely at that point that the second wind kicks in. It is the exhaustion of human ability that often triggers divine intervention.

The Spirit takes our inarticulate thoughts, unexpressed desires, ineffable perplexities, and unexplainable dilemmas. The Spirit takes our unanswerable questions, confounding riddles, bewildering ambiguities, unresolved tensions, and irreconcilable strivings. The Spirit takes all of these, sorts through them, organizes, interprets, and places them in a neat memo. Then, the Spirit ships that memo Federal Express to God's desk, so that God can do something about it.

The Spirit—the second wind—is a catalyst to move us from weakness to strength. If you are like me, God has answered some prayers in your life that you didn't even know you had prayed. The answer to the prayer surprised you because your confusion prevented you from even praying the prayer. While you were stuttering and stammering and hemming and hawing and pacing the floor because you did not know what to pray for, the Spirit interpreted your confusion. And in the Spirit's own language— what Paul calls "sighs too deep for words"—the Spirit relayed your desires to God, and God got busy on your behalf.

When helping us with our deepest human problems that we can't even voice in language, the Holy Spirit has a language to talk to God, and that language is so deep that it can't be expressed in words. Can you imagine how deep the conversation is when the Spirit talks to God and God to the Spirit? God and the Spirit communicate in their own language when helping us with our deepest dilemmas. I am so glad that the Spirit helps us in our weakness.

When verse 26 says that the Spirit helps us with our weakness, the Greek verb translated "to help" can also be translated "to lend a hand." Thus, verse 26 could be translated, "The Spirit lends us a hand in our weakness." Let me bid you good day by illustrating how the second wind—the Holy Spirit—works.

Three times a week, early in the morning, I exercise in the gym. At least twice a week I lift weights, and one of my favorite lifts is the bench press. Since I am a small-framed man, I always look around to locate the biggest, strongest person in the gym, and I ask that person to be my spotter. The spotter stands behind the bench press to ensure my safety.

The other day I put 155 pounds on the bench press and easily lifted it fifteen times. I then put on 185 pounds and pressed it ten times. Then I lifted 205 pounds five times. For my final set I had 225 pounds on the bench press bar. I pushed it up the first time with some difficulty, and the second time with great difficulty, and by the third repetition, I knew I was in trouble. I hit what weight lifters call the "sticking point"—that place where you simply can't move the weight any further. Now when 225 pounds are suspended above your chest and the law of gravity is taking effect, that's a problem! The only thing I could do was holler, "Help!"

But my spotter obviously knew something about weight lifting. When I reached the sticking point the spotter did not simply snatch the weight from me. If the spotter had snatched the weight, doing all the work for me, my muscles would not have benefited. The strain of lifting can increase strength.

Instead of grabbing the weight, the spotter ever so lightly tapped the bench press bar up. The spotter simply lent me a hand, tapping that weight until I received my second wind. When the second wind came, I was able to push through the sticking point.

Likewise, says Paul, the Spirit lends us a hand. Somebody listening to me today has reached the sticking point with some spiritual weight. If you came to church today thinking that the Spirit was going to lift all the weight for you, you are mistaken. The Spirit is our spotter. If we are humble enough to cry, "Help," the Spirit will lend us a hand, lifting that weight just enough to push us past the sticking point.

The message of hope today is that we have access to second wind—that tap that allows us to push on, to push up, and to push harder. The second wind is that spark that gives us the extra strength, that moment of relief that gives us courage to fight on. Thank God for the second wind! When my first wind runs out, the second wind kicks in.

Don't throw in the towel; wait for the second wind. Don't give up the fight; wait for the second wind. Keep on running the race; wait for the second wind. If you have struck out at the plate, keep on swinging; wait for the second wind. When the road is rough and the going gets tough, just wait for the second wind.

> Have you not known? Have you not heard? The LORD is the everlasting God, the Creator of the ends of the earth. He does not faint or grow weary; his understanding is unsearchable. He gives power to the faint, and strengthens the powerless. Even youths will faint and be weary, and the young will fall exhausted; but those who wait for the LORD shall renew their strength, they shall mount up with wings like eagles, they shall run and not be weary, they shall walk and not faint. (Isa. 40:28-31)

The contest is grueling; the battle is demanding; the game is tough; but your second wind is on the way. The days are weary and the nights are long, but just wait for the second wind. There might be anxieties in your life; battles on your job; not enough money in your pocket; and disappointment in your spirit; but wait for the second wind.

Even now, I feel the wind blowing in here. Thank you, God, for the second wind! Amen.

Theological and Rhetorical Analysis of the Sermon

This sermon developed two emphases. First, it declared God's gracious intervention in human weakness through the work of the Holy Spirit (the gospel claim of the sermon). Second, it encouraged appropriate human responses to God's grace: humble admission of weakness and patient endurance (the gospel conduct of the sermon).

Given the sermon's emphasis on the Holy Spirit, I worked to avoid two theological dangers. The first danger was "spiritual exclusivity." Language about the Holy Spirit has often been divisive in Christian traditions. Some persons have singled out a particular manifestation of the Spirit as a "litmus test" to indicate the identity of truly "Spirit-filled" people. This sermon needed to remind hearers of the inclusive ministry of the Holy Spirit. Thus, early in the sermon, I declared:

> Every child of God has access to the second wind! Ever since the church's birthday on the day of Pentecost, second wind has been available for every twice-born child of God.... The Holy Spirit is perhaps most windlike in that it is accessible to everyone but can be controlled by no one.

Second, I wanted to avoid giving any excuse for human irresponsibility. Some people mistakenly expect the Holy Spirit to serve as their substitute while they neglect their spiritual responsibilities. The intervention of the Spirit does not negate human exertion. Thus, in the sermon, I insisted:

> To wait only for the second wind without ever accessing your first wind is a manifestation of irresponsibility.... We have to do our part. Don't relegate the Holy Spirit to some kind of invisible genie that you can summon by saying the magic words.

Earlier in this book, I argued that an appropriate theology of the cross could ensure that our preaching remains faithful to the gospel. While not prominent in this sermon, a theology of the cross is, nevertheless, present in the sermon's discussion of human weakness. I attempted to engage the real struggles of my listeners, asserting:

If you are weak, or in the words of the song, if you are "weary, worn, and sad"; if you are wrestling with disappointment and despair; if the cares of finances and family are frustrating you to no end; if the death or sickness of a loved one is snatching the vitality from your life; if there is any weakness in your life; I have some advice for you. Don't give up the fight; don't throw in the towel; keep on running; keep on striding; because you might be on the verge of catching your second wind.

Potentially, the sermon might have been stronger if I had provided a poignant example of my own weakness. I chose not to include such autobiographical reflections in the body of the sermon. Instead, I inserted an autobiographical note in my final story about weight lifting. With a slight touch of humor, this concluding story served as a metaphor for a variety of human weaknesses—those moments when life's weight forces us to holler, "Help!" It is important that preachers regularly depict themselves as persons needing help and not always as persons giving help.[6]

A greater emphasis on the communal nature of the Holy Spirit might have also improved this sermon. Often Christians speak as if the Holy Spirit is a private possession. Whereas the Spirit certainly empowers individuals, the Spirit also works for and through the community. At one point, I alluded to the Spirit's communal empowerment of church:

Surely, the church needs more power!... The church without power is a social club. Praying without power is a useless monologue. A trustee board meeting without power is organized deadness. A deacon board meeting without power is pious parading. Bible study without power is a weekly book club. Singing without power is sanctimonious noise. Preaching without power is meaningless chatter. If our witness and lives are to truly make a difference for Christ, we need the power of the second wind, which is the Holy Spirit.

In spite of this brief reference, the communal aspects of the sermon remained underdeveloped. Since some of my sermons explore the importance of communal support, I chose not to accentuate that aspect in this sermon. Still, I might have provided one example of how the Holy Spirit helps us by means of the kind deeds and encouraging words of others.

Concerning passion in preaching, I recommended in chapter 1 that preachers model their pulpit behavior on God, since God radically invests God's self in our affairs. This sermon attempted to capture both God's passionate involvement in our personal struggles and the intimate connection between God and the Holy Spirit. In Romans 8, God is neither idle nor aloof. God, through the Spirit, enters deeply into our trials, and God and the Spirit have intimate conversation in their own "language."

This sermon tried to model passion in other ways as well. Through emphatic gestures and modulation of vocal tone—neither of which can be captured on paper—I demonstrated that the truth of the message had seized my soul. For instance, in the concluding story about weight lifting, I made gestures with my arms to replicate the lifting of a bench-press bar. Also, when I said, "I hit what weight lifters call the 'sticking point.'... The only thing I could do was holler, 'Help!'" I actually hollered the word *help* at the top of my voice in my sermon delivery. Thus, there was a correspondence between *what* I was saying and *how* I was saying it.

If a sermon's passion motivates listeners to take the message with them, a sermon's language and imagery provide the "to-go boxes." Admittedly, the sermon's language was occasionally sophisticated. I used phrases such as "intangible reality," and "ineffable perplexities." Whereas such phrases are natural features of my spoken and written language, I tried to limit the presence of abstract words. When such words appeared, I employed other rhetorical tools to solidify my points. Two rhetorical tools were repetition and "accumulating thought."[7]

For example, in the following section of the sermon the language was complex, but the repetition hopefully brought clarity to my point. Notice how the phrase "The Spirit takes" served as a refrain, which in the example below I have italicized.

Additionally, the repetition was an exercise in "accumulating thought"—an oral technique whereby a speaker makes the same point by rapidly offering multiple examples. In written discourse accumulating thought might appear as wordiness. A writer might inform readers simply with one example. But in a sermon the transmittance of cognitive information is never enough. A preacher must also strive for emotional impact. Thus, repetition and accumulating thought functioned as "context clues" for meaning, even when complex language was used.

> *The Spirit takes* our inarticulate thoughts, unexpressed desires, ineffable perplexities, and unexplainable dilemmas. *The Spirit takes* our unanswerable questions, confounding riddles, bewildering ambiguities, unresolved tensions, and irreconcilable strivings. *The Spirit takes* all of these, sorts through them, organizes, interprets, and places them in a neat memo. Then, the Spirit ships that memo Federal Express to God's desk, so that God can do something about it.

Two additional rhetorical tools aiding this sermon were euphony and rhythm.[8] Euphony, which is derived from Greek words meaning a "good sound," involves the combination of words for a pleasing and persuasive effect. Rhythm entails the speed at which words are uttered. Recently, a National Public Radio broadcast about jazz offered a brilliant description of rhythm—"playing around with time." Like Wynton Marsalis altering the speed of his trumpet's cadences, preachers should play around with time when voicing the phrases and sentences in their sermons. Variations in the rate of speech maintain hearers' attention and create room for hearers' active participation.

Examples of euphony in the sermon include:

> Second wind—that last little pep in your step when you were too pooped to pop.

> To use the first wind to the exclusion of the second wind is an invitation to *futility*. To wait only for the second wind without ever accessing your first wind is a manifestation of *irresponsibility*.

In the first example, the rhyming words *pep* and *step* and the words *too pooped to pop* combine to create an intriguing phrase. In the second example, the vocal stress on the last word of each sentence in my delivery—*futility* and *irresponsibility*—heightened the contrast I was establishing.

Concerning rhythm, conscious elongated pauses offer an easy way to play around with time in sermon delivery. Pauses in a sermon are similar to musical rests in a song. In the following example of rhythm, I have inserted ellipses to indicate the pause in speech. When I paused at this juncture, quite often parishioners vocally finished the sentence for me—a telling indicator that they were energetically involved in the sermon.

> Don't give up the fight; don't throw in the towel; keep on running; keep on striding; because you might be on the verge of catching your ... second wind.

My final rhetorical observations concern this sermon's introduction and conclusion. Investing significant energy into the creation of stirring, relevant beginnings and endings will bring exponential returns in the pulpit. When composing sermons, some preachers merely sketch an introduction and finalize it once the body of the sermon is complete. This is a commendable practice.

However, I always write a complete introduction first when creating a sermon. The introduction then functions as a detailed guide that compels me to ask two crucial questions: What must I say next in order to be *credible* with my listeners, and what must I leave out in order to be *tolerable* to my listeners?

Many preachers struggle more often with the second question. Based on the content and direction of their sermon introductions, they fail to identify and leave out inessential elements from their critical interpretive work. Consequently, they preach the "bloated" sermons of which I spoke in the previous chapter. Bloated sermons are intolerable to listeners and are poor stewardship of the gifts of people's attention and time.

Whereas there are many ways to introduce a sermon, I usually pose two other basic questions when composing an introduction.[9]

First, what "hook" will I use to grab and maintain people's attention? Second, how long of a hook do I need?

In "Second Wind," the hook was sports. I utilized the American fascination with athletes and athletic competition to capture and preserve people's interest. So saturated is American culture with sports coverage that even persons uninterested in athletics still know about Michael Jordan and Venus and Serena Williams.

But in my introduction, I spoke first about my own experiences in sports, even before I alluded to sports superstars. In rhetorical terms, this was an attempt to establish *ēthos*—the listeners' perceptions about the speaker's character. At the beginning of sermons, preachers introduce themselves as well as their messages. Congregants assess everything from a sermon's opening sentence to a preacher's vocal tone and personal appearance in order to determine if, and how closely, they will listen.

Given the forthcoming discussion in the sermon, I wanted my listeners to know that I was not simply an armchair quarterback. I was acquainted with and passionate about the announced topic. Additionally, the suggestion about playing professional football if I had been taller, faster, and heavier added a slight touch of humor that hopefully created goodwill among my listeners.

The hook in this sermon introduction was fairly long. In the last sentence in the second paragraph, I created suspense:

> Having been involved in athletics most of my life, I know there is a phenomenon that is every athlete's best friend and perhaps greatest asset.

By not immediately identifying this greatest asset, I prolonged the suspense. Once I identified my topic, I spent considerable time defining it to ensure that my listeners were clear about the second wind.

Then, just as my listeners were feeling comfortable with the *athletic* definition of second wind, I hinted at another *theological* meaning of second wind. Thus, the paragraph below served as the bridge between the elongated introduction and the body of the sermon. With this transitional paragraph, a new suspense was created—a suspense that the body of the sermon would address.

> You might be a weekend athlete, or you might have never participated in athletics a day in your life. Yet the message I have for you today is that you, too, can experience second wind. Second wind is not just for great athletes like Muhammad Ali, Michael Jordan, Emmett Smith, or Venus and Serena Williams. Every child of God has access to the second wind!

A more concise comment about the sermon's conclusion is fitting since I have spoken about the conclusion above. Although preachers should consider the emotional impact of every aspect of their sermons, the conclusion is an especially opportune moment to appeal to listeners' emotions. At this point, a sermon has already marshaled its main information, and the conclusion should apply one final jolt of motivation.

In two specific ways, the conclusion of "Second Wind" attempted to motivate its listeners. First, I peppered the conclusion with pithy exhortations.

> Don't give up the fight; wait for the second wind. Keep on running the race; wait for the second wind. If you have struck out at the plate, keep on swinging; wait for the second wind. When the road is rough and the going gets tough, just wait for the second wind.

Second, I appealed to the famous passage in Isaiah 40 about the renewing of strength. Many ecclesial traditions—and certainly those in African American communities—consider this Isaiah text a landmark scripture about hope and possibility. By citing this passage, I provided common ground for listeners to celebrate with me the arrival of the second wind.

More Pauline Preaching

The remainder of this chapter presents two other sermons that I have preached from Pauline texts. A colleague's critique follows each sermon. Ideally, the analyses of all three sermons in this chapter will model the internal conversations that preachers should have with themselves, and the external conversations that should occur among preachers and their listeners.

Initially, I preached a version of "Dead *and* Alive" at a Lenten service at the Bethel African Methodist Episcopal Church in Baltimore, Maryland. I am grateful to the pastor of Bethel Church, Dr. Frank M. Reid III, for the invitation to participate in that service. The present version is an adaptation preached in worship services since 2002. I preached "Hanging Loose in an Uptight World" initially at Douglas Memorial Community Church in Baltimore, Maryland, when I was the senior pastor. The present version is an adaptation preached in services since the 2001 terrorist attacks in the United States.

Dead *and* Alive
(Romans 6:1-11)

My mother is a huge fan of cowboy shows—*Bonanza*, *Gunsmoke*, and *The Rifleman*. She is so familiar with these shows that she often recites the lines along with the characters. As a boy, I would occasionally sit with my mother and watch these shows. I soon discovered that the characterization and underlying plot structure in these programs seemed to remain fairly constant.

On the one hand, there were the law-abiding citizens of Dodge, and the chief protector of Dodge was the sheriff or the United States marshal. On the other hand, there was the law-breaking bank robber. In the "moral universe" of the cowboy shows, there were few shades of gray. Things were black and white, cut-and-dried. The sheriff was clean-shaven and rode a white horse. The bank robber had a scraggly beard and rode a black horse. On the one side, you had the Lone Ranger, and on the other, you had Jesse James or Billy the Kid.

And, of course, the plot structure was utterly predictable. The bad guy robs the bank and runs from the law. The robber shoots and pillages, leading the law on a wild chase through the wild, wild West. This chase might continue for three-fourths of the show, but when the deal came down, the sheriff always apprehended his man. We knew that he would. The question was *how* would he catch him.

As the fugitive cowboy led the sheriff on a wild chase, the sheriff would put up posters all over the countryside. The poster would have a picture of the fugitive, and underneath the picture in big bold letters would be the words: **"Wanted: Dead or Alive."**

The poster suggested that this bad cowboy was such a menace to society that he had to be stopped. If stopping him meant killing him, that was acceptable and within the confines of the law. The criminal was wanted dead *or* alive. In other words, by any means necessary, we want him. Dead *or* alive. Put him in jail, or put him in a casket. We don't care. We just want this criminal. We want him dead *or* alive.

Now the two letters *o* and *r* between "Dead *or* Alive" create a coordinating conjunction that introduces an alternative possibility. Dead *or* alive. There are two alternatives. There is no middle ground. It has to be one way or the other. The conjunction "or" means that if we choose one alternative, we automatically refuse the other. If we bring him in dead, he is not alive. If we bring him in alive, he is not dead. The sheriff did not care which mutually exclusive option we chose. He just wanted the criminal apprehended. Dead *or* alive is how the sheriff wanted the menacing cowboy in those old shows.

But according to my reading of Romans 6, God wants the Christian dead *and* alive. The sheriff wants the criminal dead *or* alive, but the Savior wants the Christian dead *and* alive.

In Romans 6:11, Paul declares, "So you also must consider yourselves dead to sin *and* alive to God in Christ." Some translations have, "dead *but* alive." Yet, I believe the New Revised Standard Version has the better theological nuance when it translates the phrase, "dead *and* alive." In the life of the Christian, death and life are supposed to happen simultaneously:

"We must consider ourselves dead to sin *and* alive to God in Christ."

Romans 6:1-11 is a "wanted poster." It is an advertisement from God to capture not criminals, but Christians who are ready and willing to embody the ethical implications of life in Christ. The Savior wants us dead *and* alive.

But how can this be? Life is the antithesis to death. Dead *and* alive is a nonsensical statement; it's oxymoronic. Dead *and* alive? That statement consists of two contradictory ideas trying to occupy the same semantic space. One of Paul's goals in Romans is to fathom the depths of this seeming contradiction.

In Romans, Paul demonstrates that everybody is under the power of Sin—both the Gentiles and the Jews. Generally in Romans, when Paul mentions Sin, he is not talking so much about sin as an individual act of disobedience or bad behavior.[10] He is talking about Sin as a cosmic power.

In other words, he is talking about Sin with a capital S. Sin, as a cosmic force, is a tyrant that rules over the believer like a despotic monarch. Sin with a capital S is what creates sin with a lower case s.

In Romans, Paul declares that there is a wicked force in the world that willfully opposes the ways of God. Everyone has experienced this tyrannical force at one time or another. It whispers in your ear and tells you to lie to your spouse. It's that internal voice that makes you jealous when God blesses other people in a different and seemingly better way than God blesses you. It's that voice that tells you that you are not gossiping when you talk about other people's business; you are just keeping your friends "informed." There is a malevolent force out there, and Paul calls it Sin.

Regrettably, Sin has left its characteristic mark on every life. Sin's distinctive signature is spiritual death. The good news of Romans 6, however, is that there is a way to break the curse of Sin. Ironically, the curse of Sin is broken through death.

In other words, we must fight fire with fire. Sin rules over us like a tyrant, and it brings death. The only way to break free from the death of Sin is through death—dying, not in the natural realm, but in the spiritual realm.

For Paul, baptism is a powerful symbol of dying to Sin in the spiritual realm. Romans 6 contains Paul's reflection on the ethical implications of baptism. Baptism equals death. Listen to Paul in Romans 6:3: "Do you not know that all of us who have been baptized into Christ Jesus were baptized into his death?" In Romans 6, Paul reminds his hearers of the significance of their baptism.

To be baptized by the Holy Spirit into fellowship with Christ is like a spiritual Fourth of July. Baptism into Christ is Independence Day. Baptism into Christ represents that moment when we break free from the hostile power of Sin, no longer being held captive by its seductive power.

According to Paul, believers through their baptism share symbolically in Christ's death. Baptism is likened to Christ's death because it signifies our willingness to have our carnal nature crucified. There is a tendency in us to idolize ourselves while failing to glorify God. This tendency must be eliminated so that our transformed spiritual nature might arise in us, leading us to give God the glory that God deserves.

Sin, like a parasite, is only able to survive if it possesses a host body. Our carnal nature provides a suitable environment for Sin to fester. Yet baptism symbolizes the death of that carnal nature. By annihilating Sin's host body—our carnal nature—we render Sin innocuous.

Paul declares that after we have been "buried" by baptism into Christ's death, we are dead to Sin. Now, I want to be abundantly clear on a point. To be dead to Sin does not mean that we never again transgress. As long as we are in this life, we are prone to making mistakes—mistakes for which we can sincerely seek pardon.

Our death to Sin, however, should indicate that we are no longer *dominated* by Sin. Once we have been baptized into Christ, Sin no longer should have dominion over us. Sin should no longer rule over us because now we have divinely bestowed authority over Sin.

As we mature in Christ, our moral stumbling blocks should progressively become stepping-stones for us to move higher in our fellowship with Christ. But in order for this to happen, we must be dead to sin *and* alive to God in Christ. Paul says in verse 4 that when we are alive to God in Christ, we will walk in the *newness* of life. When we are dead *and* alive, there ought to be newness about us. The African American saints of my childhood used to testify that after they met Jesus, "they looked at their hands, and their hands looked new. They looked at their feet, and they did, too."

Christians who are dead to Sin *and* alive to Christ don't do the same old stuff; don't talk the same old junk; don't think the same old ungodly thoughts. When we are dead to sin *and* alive to Christ, we should start singing a new theme song: "What a wonderful change in my life has been wrought, since Jesus came into my heart."

When we are dead *and* alive, personal transformations are bound to occur. Sadly, I have known some people who have been in church most of their lives, but they have never been changed. It is tragic, indeed, to know the language, hymns, prayers, and liturgical moments of the church without ever experiencing the transformation that results from being in Christ.

I have seen some people in church get caught up in the excitement of worship and begin to dance. Yet, unless they experience a death to Sin, they are simply dancing devils. When we are dead *and* alive, we are ever reminded that the chief goal of the Holy Spirit is not excitement but transformation. When we are dead *and* alive, God's Spirit on the inside of us starts working on the outside of us, and there will be a change in our lives!

If we take seriously Paul's words in Romans 6, every day there should be a funeral in the life of the Christian. None of us has been completely conformed to the image of God, but every day we ought to lay to rest something that is not like God, which hinders us from having a closer walk with God.

What do we need to lay to rest today? What do we need to bury at this very hour? Do we need to bury a bad attitude, jealousy, animosity, an unforgiving spirit, doubt, a sense of shame, or feelings of inadequacy?

I am persuaded that in this worship service a host of funerals are about to take place. Some folk are preparing to bury their old selves. Quickly, let us call all the morticians in town, and tell them to come immediately to this church![11] Their professional services are needed—folk are burying sinful elements of themselves even as I speak!

In the choir stand, someone just buried a three-year-old grudge. On the deacons' pew, someone just buried an inflexible personality. In this pulpit, someone just buried an inflated ego.

If there is something that is prohibiting your spiritual growth, I dare you to look it squarely in the eye and say, "Earth to earth, ashes to ashes, dust to dust. Rest in peace!"

At the same time that we are burying the negative, we ought to celebrate the glorious resurrection of the positive realities of Christ in us. In Christ, funerals are always penultimate. Death is but a comma in salvation's story. The resurrection is the final exclamation point!

Through the power of the resurrection, I am ever alive to God and to my neighbor. Because of the resurrection, Paul tells us in Romans 12 that we are living sacrifices. Sacrifices are normally dead. In the sense that we have been crucified with Christ, we are a sacrifice. Yet we are not dead sacrifices; we are living sacrifices. We are dead *and* alive.

This nonsensical stuff of being dead *and* alive is not just in Romans. Its echoes are elsewhere in scripture. In Galatians 2:19-20, Paul declares, "I have been crucified with Christ; and it is no longer I who live, but it is Christ who lives in me." In Colossians 3:2-3, the writer exclaims, "Set your minds on things that are above.... For you have died, and your life is hidden with Christ in God."

I am dead *and* alive. I am dead to sin *and* alive in Christ. Thank God that the resurrected Christ lives in me. Christ lives! In the words of the Alfred H. Ackley hymn "He Lives": "You ask me how I know He lives? He lives within my heart." Amen.

A Colleague's Critique: Gail R. O'Day

Gail R. O'Day is A. H. Shatford Professor of New Testament and Preaching and Associate Dean of Academic Affairs at Candler School

*of Theology, Emory University, in Atlanta, Georgia. She is the author
of the John commentary in* The New Interpreter's Bible *and the general editor of the* Journal of Biblical Literature.

The singular strength of this sermon is the way in which it
takes the text of Romans 6:1-11 as its shaping conversation partner. Braxton does not begin his work with a preconceived theological or pastoral goal and then search for a biblical text on
which to hang that goal. The theological richness and pastoral
imperatives that emerge from Paul's words set the direction for
this sermon.

Romans 6:1-11 is shaped around three questions that Paul
poses to the Roman church, and these questions also shape the
structure of Braxton's sermon. The first question (v. 1) is rhetorical, the anticipated answer made clear by Paul's, "By no means!"
(v. 2a). The second question is harder, and the one around which
the first part of the body of Braxton's sermon is formed: "How can
we who died to sin go on living in it?" (v. 2b). In line with this
question, the sermon names sin theologically (sin as a cosmic
force) and identifies how that cosmic force is in evidence in people's daily lives. Braxton leads his hearers to see that no one, or
any part of the cosmos, is exempt from the death-dealing power
of sin. To use Paul's words, he shows the ways that Christians
continue to live in sin, despite the presence of grace.

Paul's third question ("Do you not know that all of us who have
been baptized into Christ were baptized into his death?") marks
the turn in Romans 6:1-11 from diagnosis to proclamation.
Braxton follows Paul's theological and pastoral lead and moves his
listeners to remember their baptism and to see baptism as the antidote to the power of sin and death. As Braxton rightly emphasizes,
there is a deep paradox here, because Paul presents baptism as a
form of death that undercuts the deathly power of sin.

Once the sermon makes this turn with Paul, Braxton con-
structs word pictures of how the power of sin can be declared
dead through the power of baptism and the newness of life that it
brings. The vivid metaphor of the funeral effectively and memo-
rably communicates that sin can really die through baptism.

This sermon asks the listeners to see their lives through a theo-logical lens and shows how that lens can make a difference in the way they construe their lives. Yet Braxton's examples of sin all focus on individual behavior and individual piety. Examples of sin as a corporate or social reality might have deepened and expanded the picture.

As the above discussion indicates, the sermon models how a biblical text can provide a sermon with its form as well as its con-tent. The only exception to this is the introduction, which is not so clearly derived from the world of Romans 6:1-11. The exten-sive discussion of the predictability and conventionality of Westerns in the introduction led me to assume that predictabil-ity was a key theme for the sermon, yet that theme never resounded outside of the introduction, nor is predictability an obvious part of the fabric of the Pauline text.

The introduction is engaging, and I am sure is very engaging when the sermon is actually preached, but the sermon that follows is richer than this introduction. The metaphor system of death and funerals that Braxton uses so effectively in the last third of the ser-mon could have been used just as effectively in an introduction to set up the notion of dead *and* alive and would have oriented the lis-tener more quickly to the focus and direction of this fine sermon.

Hanging Loose in an Uptight World
Philippians 4:6-7

There is a killer on the loose. Law enforcement agencies have never succeeded in tracking this killer down. Having never been arrested or indicted, this killer has no "rap sheet" and has never served a day in prison. This killer, nonetheless, has aided and abetted in the deaths of countless people.

There is a killer on the loose. This killer possesses no weapons of mass destruction nor totes an automatic firearm. Even so, this killer has mowed down and maimed men, women, and children from a variety of cultures. This killer has covertly escaped detection by the most advanced scientific and military surveillance technology. We all need to be very aware because this killer might have targeted one of us.

As I have described this killer, I am not sure what face or name has come to your mind. The killer I have in mind is *stress*. Do not fool yourself. Stress can be lethal! Recently, some psychiatrists have coined a term, *toxic worry*. This term—*toxic worry*—suggests that stress can set in motion physiological and psychological processes that might contribute directly or indirectly to our dysfunction and destruction. Stress is a formidable foe not to be taken lightly.

In these tumultuous days of international warfare and heated rhetoric among estranged nations, there is much public conversation about mass murderers and "enemies of the state." Two names come quickly to mind: Osama Bin Laden and Saddam Hussein. As a citizen of this country, I want to know who are the "enemies of the state." Yet, as a Christian theologian and a citizen of another invisible commonwealth, I also want to know who are the "enemies of the soul."

It is the politician's primary responsibility to warn American citizens about the enemies of the state. It is the preacher's primary responsibility to warn kingdom citizens about the enemies of the soul. Stress is an enemy of the soul that attempts to violently snatch from each of us our security, our joy, and our very lives. I personally cannot always grapple directly with the enemies of the state. But as a child of God I can frequently engage in a more direct offensive against the enemies of the soul.

Don't misunderstand me. As Christians, we should take a vested interest in national and global affairs. Today, however, my focus is much more local and individual. My primary goal is not to speak about international affairs but to address our individual anxieties.

The zip codes to which I am mailing this sermon are local. This sermon is not concerned primarily about what is happening in the White House. I want to address what's going on in *your house*. In our frenzy about external murderers, let us not forget those foes that "do us in" from the inside.

Stress can be a killer. Unaware to you, the vicious invisible hands of stress may be strangling your life away. Stress frequently incapacitates many of us mentally, physically, and spiritually.

In this church, stress has its hands around some people's necks so tightly that they can't even think straight. You are in church right now, dressed up, singing the hymns, praying the prayers, listening to this sermon, but your mind is a thousand miles from here because you are stressed out. Some of you want to smile, but stress has apparently paralyzed those muscles that facilitate smiling, and all you can muster is a menacing frown.

All of us are stressed about a million matters. Stress has been around as long as humans have been around. Yet it seems that in a "post 9-11 world," stress levels have risen exponentially. Since September 11, 2001, a whole new set of anxieties and fears has been added to our lists.

Some are more squeamish than ever about boarding airplanes. Some are still anxious to open mail, fearing that they, too, might meet their death in the dust of anthrax. Many are nervously watching the plummet of the stock market, wondering if they will have to trade their Wall Street address for a shanty on skid row.

And these more recent anxieties do not even begin to exhaust the countless other worries that daily deplete life from us: What does my boss think about me? Can I complete this job or school assignment on time and still get at least two hours of sleep? Who will keep the kids while I am at work? Should I place my mother in a nursing home? Where is the money coming from to pay this bill? Will I ever find a true soul mate? The list of stressors seems endless.

The pain you are feeling in your body might not be bursitis or arthritis; it might be stress. A physician once told me that stress, this vicious killer, usually attacks the vulnerable places in our bodies. Consequently, stress goes to the creases—the places where there are joints. The crick in your back might have less to do with your hard mattress and more to do with the madness in your mind.

Stress makes you uptight and irritable. The only thing worse than being uptight is being around other folk who are uptight.

Take a minute and scan your pew, and see if you can spot any uptight people. There are uptight people in every family, church, and community. I am convinced that we live in an uptight world.

Psychiatrists and psychologists have long discussed the harmful effects of stress. My sermon title is from a psychology book that I once encountered. In 1974, Dr. Ken Olson, a psychologist, wrote a best-selling book entitled *The Art of Hanging Loose in an Uptight World*. Three decades ago, this psychologist diagnosed our world as uptight. Today his diagnosis is no less accurate than it was thirty years ago.

Examining his book, I realized that stress is not simply a psychological or physiological problem. Stress is also a theological problem. Stress is a spiritual malady. God never intended for us to inhabit an uptight world. An existence typified by anxiety was not the Creator's design. Thus, in order to counteract the deadly effects of stress, we need some "soul medicine."

Nearly twenty centuries before Dr. Olson wrote his popular book, the apostle Paul wrote a book—Philippians—instructing people how to hang loose in an uptight world. At the sermon's inception I read Paul's prescription, but let me read it again:

> Do not worry about anything, but in everything by prayer and supplication with thanksgiving let your requests be made known to God. And the peace of God, which surpasses all understanding, will guard your hearts and your minds in Christ Jesus.

Skeptics might assume that Paul's words are simply pie-in-the-sky rhetoric written by someone unacquainted with life in the raw. The historical details surrounding this letter, however, prove such an assumption to be inaccurate.

Paul composes this letter while under arrest and in prison. He was imprisoned for the capital offense of proclaiming the anti-imperial, anti-establishment message of Jesus Christ. Paul is not reclining on "flowery beds of ease." On the contrary, Paul is in jail and in a real jam. You might even say that he is in a tight situation. For him, it's tight, but he refuses to be *uptight*.

From prison, he declares: "Do not worry about anything, but in everything by prayer and supplication with thanksgiving let your requests be made known to God." Or if Paul were to give a contemporary paraphrase of his ancient words, he might exclaim: "Y'all hang loose in an uptight world!"

When Paul exhorts us to avoid worrying, he is not advocating that we become aloof to the pressing matters of our daily lives. We ought to be concerned about and passionately involved in the quest to maximize our talents and experiences.

Yet there is a fine line between concern and preoccupation. It's a short step from having an interest in your life to making an idol god out of your life. Paul is urging us to avoid the fretful preoccupation with our welfare that wraps around our spirits, constricting our ability to glorify God and to show deep compassion for others.

Meditating on Paul's exhortation in verse 6, I asked God to reveal to me a portable definition of worry. Here's what I received: *Worry is a demonically induced deception that causes us to mistake our dilemmas for our destinies.* Surely, there are some people in this church who are equating their dilemmas and their destinies.

Our dilemmas can contribute to or even impinge upon our divinely directed destinies, but they can never ultimately derail our destinies. Christ has guaranteed the destination of our trip. Thus, we can wear more loosely the concerns that have caused us to be so uptight. It is possible to hang loose in an uptight world, neutralizing the lethal consequences of toxic worry. According to Paul, the antidote is profoundly simple and simply profound: prayer.

Prayer is the prescription. Prayer is the key. Prayer is the answer. In verse 6, there is a marvelous parallelism. In the first clause, Paul says, "Worry about nothing." He begins the second clause by exclaiming, "but in everything with prayer." Did you catch it? Worry about *no* thing. Pray about *every* thing.

So crucial is prayer to hanging loose in an uptight world that Paul employs three different Greek words for prayer in this one verse. Although the words are very similar and should not be distinguished too intensely, each word contains a nuance that I would like to explore briefly. How do we hang loose, Paul? Paul responds, "Learn how to engage in three kinds of praying."

The first Greek word that Paul uses in verse 6 for prayer (*proseuchē*) connotes prayer offered as an act of worship or devotion to God. If we are going to hang loose in an uptight world, worship should not be a *place* we go once a week on Sunday; it should be a *prayerful posture* we assume every moment of our lives.

If the only time we pray is when our eyes are closed, we are forfeiting our power. Worshipful prayer is often best accomplished with our eyes wide open—both the eyes on our faces and the eyes on our souls. Worshipful prayer occurs when we reverently view every circumstance in our lives in the context of our relationship with God.

Noted scholar Krister Stendahl has admirably captured the meaning of prayer as worship. He once told the story of a little boy who kept following his mother around the house from one room to another. Finally, the mother turned to her son and said, "What do you want?" The boy responded, "Nothing, Mama, I just want to be where you are."

Prayer as worship is to say to our divine parent, "Mama God, Daddy God, I just want to be where you are." When we develop that kind of prayer life—prayer as worship—it's hard to stay uptight for long.

In verse 6 Paul also uses a second word for prayer (*deēsis*) that is often translated "petition" or "supplication." This word connotes prayer as an earnest expression of human need. This kind of prayer reminds us that we can't make it on our own. This kind of prayer shatters the myth of "self-sufficiency." This kind of prayer keeps us humbly reaching up to God and out to people. Many people are uptight because they are too proud to admit they have needs. Our admission *of* needs is often our admission *into* God's power.

Then in verse 6 Paul uses a third word for prayer (*aitēma*) that is often translated "request." This word refers to more than the general recognition of our need of God. Instead, it connotes a very specific, concrete naming of the things we need.

As children of God, it is our right and privilege to ask God for the particular, concrete blessings that we need. But please notice the order. It's only when we pray just to be in God's presence and pray as a basic expression of our dependence on God that we can specifically ask God for the right things.

Moreover, in this passage Paul teaches that thanksgiving should characterize every aspect of our prayer lives. It's hard to be uptight when we really take a look at our stockroom of blessings. Have you sent God a thank-you note lately for your inventory of blessings? Just in case you haven't, let's send God some thank-you notes right now:

> Thank you, Lord, because the blood is still running warm in my veins. Thank you, Lord, for waking me up this morning in my right mind in spite of the situations that tried to make me lose my mind. Thank you, Lord, for a place to lie down last night. Thank you, Lord, for a family who loves me in spite of my crazy ways. Thank you, Lord, for the visual wonder of a morning sunrise. Thank you, Lord, for the cool moisture that comes on the wings of the morning dew. Thank you, Lord, for my job. My boss may be tough, but at least I have some place to work. Thank you, Lord, for giving me another chance. Now I know for sure that you deal with us according to mercy and not justice.[12]

To hang loose, pray frequently and pray fervently. In verse 7, Paul declares, "And the peace of God, which surpasses all understanding, will *guard* your hearts and your minds in Christ Jesus."

The verb "to guard" introduces a military metaphor. This verb suggests that the peace of God that comes from prayer will stand watch over our hearts and minds like an attentive soldier. When we pray right, the peace of God protects the precincts of our souls from invasion by unsavory characters.

As this sermon began, we posted an "all-points bulletin" on stress, the felon who uses deadly force. As this sermon concludes, we can rest more easily. Good news! God's peace—our soul's security detail—has apprehended and detained stress.

The enemy of our soul has been neutralized. Let God's people shout: "I've got peace like a river; I've got peace like a river; I've got peace like a river in my soul!" Amen.

A Colleague's Critique: Nigel D. Alston

Nigel D. Alston is a motivational speaker, columnist, Dale Carnegie and Development Dimensions International certified trainer, and radio talk-show host in Winston-Salem, North Carolina.

I like this sermon. It is a real-world message for real world anxieties, experienced by real people. And the solution it offers, to address our daily fears and uncertainties, is simple: Prayer.

Whereas the answer is simple, the application of the medicine is not as one-dimensional as one might think. Instead, it is a course of action that recognizes first things first: the presence of God; a dependence on God; and our request(s) to God.

Reading a sermon is quite different from experiencing it in person. You don't have the benefit of the style of the preacher, the nuances in delivery, and an interaction with the congregation. Together they are more than the individual parts. Reading requires an active use of the imagination to be moved and inspired to act. This sermon aids the mind's eye with its images, illustrations, and all too real descriptions of daily life to which one can relate.

As a person who speaks frequently, reads extensively, and studies those who are successful at communicating effectively, I also recognize the importance of an effective opening and closing in a speech (a sermon in this case). They are critical points, like the takeoff and landing of an airplane. If you don't handle them right, you are in big trouble.

"There is a killer on the loose" grabs your attention immediately. The stage is set. You want to know more about this elusive assassin. And it lands in an equally dramatic way: "The enemy of the soul has been neutralized." Case closed!

I can literally hear people saying, "Go ahead preacher. Amen!" I can see uptight people, myself included, sitting in the pews with fingerprints of stress imprinted around their necks.

The transitions employed—using this image of a "killer on the loose," stress and its toxic nature, and how it manifests itself in our everyday lives—are seamlessly intermingled in the message, marching you toward Paul's remedy.

It is a personal message, directed to my zip code, placed in my mailbox, and answers that important question we all have: What's in it for me?

What's the benefit? I believe it is a model, an example of one (Paul) who practiced hanging loose in a very uptight world. The case is made convincingly that we live in an uptight world, as Paul did. His situation earned him the right, through his actions, to tell us what to do in similar situations.

Don't worry. Pray about everything. Be thankful and assured that "Christ has guaranteed the destination of our trip." Our current situation is not our ultimate destiny.

This sermon represents a clear understanding of Paul's surroundings and the significance of the power of prayer in how we manage our daily affairs. The call to action—pray. If you do, you can "hang loose in an uptight world."

CHAPTER SIX

A Bibliographic Guide for Preaching Paul

Resources on the apostle Paul multiply so rapidly that it is challenging to stay abreast of Pauline scholarship. This bibliographic chapter attempts to provide a reliable path into and through the dense thicket of Pauline studies.

First, this chapter provides a selected Pauline bibliography for busy ministers. I cite a few resources that line my own bookshelves or the books in libraries that I frequently use. I include commentaries for each of the authentic Pauline Letters, several introductory biblical studies textbooks, and Web sites. As a busy minister myself, I know well the value of developing a set of trustworthy resources.

I consider the books in my personal library as "friends." Thus, to open a book is to begin or to renew a friendship. Cultivating relationships with our books can enrich our preaching ministries immeasurably.

I do not always agree with the "friends" who reside in my library. Consensus with a book is not my primary criterion for friendship. Of chief importance for me is respect. Even if I do not necessarily agree with a book's perspective, I will begin a friendship if I can at least *respect* the depth and power of its argument. The following list introduces readers to some of my most respected and distinguished "friends."

Second, I offer an annotated bibliography of some influential writings on the apostle Paul. To prevent this annotated list from being overwhelming, I have provided boundaries. First, I imposed a chronological boundary by limiting the bibliography to scholarship written from the last half of the twentieth century to the present. Second, I imposed a numerical boundary by limiting the references to twenty. This number offers a substantial yet manageable introduction for persons interested in pursuing Pauline studies further.

This annotated bibliography is the result of collaboration. I contacted several leading New Testament scholars and asked them to cite five of the most important books or essays in Pauline scholarship over the last half century. I encouraged them especially to mention works that set or altered the interpretive and theological agenda. I am grateful to Professors Jouette Bassler, Judith Gundry-Volf, Beverly Roberts Gaventa, Carl Holladay, and Carolyn Osiek for their assistance in compiling this bibliography. Collectively, they provided sixteen different references, and I added four to the list.

A Selected Pauline Bibliography for Busy Ministers

Biblical Commentaries

Romans

Byrne, Brendan. *Romans*. Collegeville, Minn.: Liturgical Press, 1996.

Dunn, James D. G. *Romans*. 2 vols. Dallas: Word Books, 1988.

Moo, Douglas. *The Epistle to the Romans*. Grand Rapids: William B. Eerdmans, 1997.

Wright, N. T. "The Letter to the Romans." In *The New Interpreter's Bible*. Vol. 10. Nashville: Abingdon Press, 2002.

1 Corinthians

Fee, Gordon D. *The First Epistle to the Corinthians*. Grand Rapids: William B. Eerdmans, 1987.

Hays, Richard B. *First Corinthians*. Louisville: Westminster John Knox Press, 1997.

Horsley, Richard A. *1 Corinthians*. Nashville: Abingdon Press, 1998.

Sampley, J. Paul. "The First Letter to the Corinthians." In *The New Interpreter's Bible*. Vol. 10. Nashville: Abingdon Press, 2002.

Witherington, Ben, III. *Conflict and Community in Corinth: A Socio-Rhetorical Commentary on 1 and 2 Corinthians*. Grand Rapids: William B. Eerdmans, 1995.

2 Corinthians

Furnish, Victor Paul. *II Corinthians*. Garden City, N.Y.: Doubleday, 1984.

Martin, Ralph P. *2 Corinthians*. Waco, Tex.: Word Books, 1986.

Murphy-O'Connor, Jerome. *The Theology of the Second Letter to the Corinthians*. Cambridge: Cambridge University Press, 1991.

Sampley, J. Paul. "The Second Letter to the Corinthians." In *The New Interpreter's Bible*. Vol. 11. Nashville: Abingdon Press, 2000.

Galatians

Betz, Hans Dieter. *Galatians*. Philadelphia: Fortress Press, 1979.

Hays, Richard B. "The Letter to the Galatians." In *The New Interpreter's Bible*. Vol. 11. Nashville: Abingdon Press, 2000.

Longenecker, Richard N. *Galatians*. Dallas: Word Books, 1990.

Martyn, J. Louis. *Galatians*. New York: Doubleday, 1997.

Williams, Sam K. *Galatians*. Nashville: Abingdon Press, 1997.

Philippians

Craddock, Fred B. *Philippians*. Louisville: Westminster John Knox Press, 1997.

Hooker, Morna D. "The Letter to the Philippians." In *The New Interpreter's Bible*. Vol. 11. Nashville: Abingdon Press, 2000.

O'Brien, Peter T. *The Epistle to the Philippians*. Grand Rapids: William B. Eerdmans, 1991.

Osiek, Carolyn. *Philippians, Philemon*. Nashville: Abingdon Press, 2000.

1 Thessalonians

Gaventa, Beverly Roberts. *First and Second Thessalonians*. Louisville: Westminster/John Knox Press, 1998.

Jewett, Robert. *The Thessalonian Correspondence*. Philadelphia: Fortress Press, 1986.

Smith, Abraham. "The First Letter to the Thessalonians." In *The New Interpreter's Bible*. Vol. 11. Nashville: Abingdon Press, 2000.

Philemon

Callahan, Allen D. *Embassy of Onesimus: The Letter of Paul to Philemon*. Valley Forge, Pa.: Trinity Press, 1997.

Dunn, James D. G. *The Epistles to the Colossians and to Philemon*. Grand Rapids: William B. Eerdmans, 1996.

Felder, Cain Hope. "The Letter to Philemon." In *The New Interpreter's Bible*. Vol. 11. Nashville: Abingdon Press, 2000.

Biblical Studies Introductions and Backgrounds

Brown, Raymond E. *An Introduction to the New Testament*. New York: Doubleday, 1997.

Ehrman, Bart D. *The New Testament: A Historical Introduction to the Early Christian Writings*. 3d ed. New York: Oxford University Press, 2004.

Ferguson, Everett. *Backgrounds of Early Christianity*. 3d ed. Grand Rapids: William B. Eerdmans, 2003.

Hawthorne, Gerald F., Ralph P. Martin, and Daniel G. Reid, eds. *Dictionary of Paul and His Letters*. Downers Grove, Ill.: InterVarsity Press, 1993.

Johnson, Luke Timothy. *The Writings of the New Testament*. Rev. ed. Minneapolis: Fortress Press, 1999.

Oden, Thomas C., gen. ed. *Ancient Christian Commentary on Scripture*. Vols. 6–9. Downers Grove, Ill.: InterVarsity Press, 1998.

Schiffman, Lawrence H. *From Text to Tradition: A History of Second Temple Rabbinic Judaism*. Hoboken, N.J.: KTAV Publishing House, 1991.

_____. *Texts and Traditions: A Source Reader for the Study of Second Temple and Rabbinic Judaism*. Hoboken, N.J.: KTAV Publishing House, 1998.

Williams, David J. *Paul's Metaphors: Their Context and Character*. Peabody, Mass.: Hendrickson Publishers, 1999.

Interpretive Theory

Braxton, Brad R. *No Longer Slaves: Galatians and African American Experience*. Collegeville, Minn.: Liturgical Press, 2002.

Felder, Cain Hope, ed. *Stony the Road We Trod: African American Biblical Interpretation*. Minneapolis: Fortress Press, 1991.

Fiorenza, Elisabeth Schüssler. *Wisdom Ways: Introducing Feminist Biblical Interpretation*. Maryknoll, N.Y.: Orbis, 2001.

González, Justo L. *Santa Biblia: The Bible Through Hispanic Eyes*. Nashville: Abingdon Press, 1996.

Green, Joel B., ed. *Hearing the New Testament: Strategies for Interpretation*. Grand Rapids: William B. Eerdmans, 1995.

McKenzie, Steven L., and Stephen R. Haynes, eds. *To Each Its Own Meaning: Biblical Criticisms and Their Application*. Revised and expanded edition. Louisville: Westminster John Knox Press, 1999.

Newsome, Carol A., and Sharon Ringe, eds. *Women's Bible Commentary*. Expanded edition. Louisville: Westminster John Knox Press, 1998.

Segovia, Fernando F. *Decolonizing Biblical Studies: A View from the Margins*. Maryknoll, N.Y.: Orbis, 2000.

Sugirtharajah, R. S. *Asian Biblical Hermeneutics and Postcolonialism: Contesting the Interpretations*. Maryknoll, N.Y.: Orbis, 1998.

Web Sites

Given the abundance and diverse quality of scripture Web sites, I recommend preachers to bookmark a few reliable sites. Otherwise, precious time that should be devoted to sermonic study is wasted in continual searching for new scripture Web sites. I only use two scripture Web sites on a regular basis. They are so comprehensive and well linked to other sites that they adequately supplement the above resources.

http://www.ntgateway.com

http://academics.smcvt.edu/pcouture

A Selected Annotated Bibliography of Significant Studies on Paul

Beker, J. Christiaan. *Paul the Apostle: The Triumph of God in Life and Thought*. Philadelphia: Fortress Press, 1980.

This book attempts to understand the whole Paul by addressing major themes of Paul's gospel. The primary theme addressed is apocalyptic. Apocalyptic was a complex worldview prevalent in Judaism and early Christianity, contending that God revealed the ultimate plans for the world through media such as dreams, visions, and other significant events.

Upon becoming an apostle of Jesus Christ, Paul believed that Christ's death and resurrection were chief revelatory moments indicating the dawning victory of God and the imminent redemption of the created order through Christ. Other themes treated in the book include: sin and death, the Jewish Law, salvation, life in Christ, the church, and the destiny of Israel. Beker focuses primarily on Galatians and Romans.

Cosgrove, Charles H. *Elusive Israel: The Puzzle of Election in Romans*. Louisville: Westminster John Knox Press, 1997.

This book raises an important question: How should Christians understand biblical texts that offer competing plausible interpretations? More specifically, Cosgrove explores the ambiguity surrounding Paul's understanding of the identity of Israel in Romans.

Furthermore, this book creates a fictitious conversation between three ancient Roman Christians who hold three different views of the interpretation of the Letter to the Romans. These views see the real Israel as consisting of: (1) individuals in the church, both Jews and Gentiles; (2) Jewish persons defined by genealogy and the practice of the Law; and (3) a select group of Jews who have believed the gospel message. Readers interested in the contemporary dialogue between Jews and Christians might find Cosgrove's book particularly illuminating.

Davies, W. D. *Paul and Rabbinic Judaism*. London: SPCK, 1955.

This book investigates those aspects of Judaism that would have influenced Paul. Whereas Paul fully embraced Christ, Davies maintains that Paul was also significantly tied to his Jewish background and identity. Paul could not and did not divorce himself from that background and identity. According to Davies, Paul did not consider the arrival of Christ as the beginning of a new religion. On the contrary, Christ's ministry signaled the arrival of the final form of Judaism and the dawning of the longed-for messianic age.

Dunn, James D. G. *The Theology of Paul the Apostle*. Grand Rapids: William B. Eerdmans, 1998.

This book explores Paul's theology, taking a particular interest in the role of religious practices and ethics in Paul's ministry. The book argues that there is a larger structure in Paul's theology than is apparent in smaller sections of his letters. Dunn depends upon the framework of Romans for this study, claiming that Romans contains Paul's preferred sequence of theological themes. Key topics treated in the book include: God, humanity, Christ, salvation, the church, and ethics.

Insisting that hostile readings of Paul are not helpful, Dunn interprets Paul sympathetically, especially in light of the modern Jewish-Christian dialogue. For Dunn, Paul was thoroughly Jewish and believed that Jesus was God's chosen one enabling salvation through the cross.

Elliott, Neil. *Liberating Paul: The Justice of God and the Politics of the Apostle.* Maryknoll, N.Y.: Orbis, 1994.

Elliott insists that Paul was an advocate of human liberation in need of liberation from the oppressive interpretations of his letters that have plagued theological scholarship for centuries. The book is divided into two parts.

In part one, Elliott explores how previous interpreters have misread Paul's Letters. According to Elliott, the deutero-Pauline Letters deserve much of the blame for this misreading of the historical Paul. Elliott argues that the deutero-Pauline Letters were so far removed from Paul's own teachings that they can be labeled as pseudo-Pauline writings. In part two, Elliott presents his reading of Paul's liberating theology. This theology was grounded in Jesus' crucifixion as a sign of solidarity with the oppressed. Those interested in the relationship between biblical scholarship and contemporary social justice issues might find this book especially useful.

Fitzmyer, Joseph A. *Romans.* New York: Doubleday, 1993.

Though supported by exhaustive research and filled with extensive bibliographies, this commentary on Romans remains manageable. Fitzmyer investigates Romans according to the standard commentary format. He addresses various sociohistorical issues surrounding the composition of Romans. He then explicates the letter under the following rubrics: doctrinal section, hortatory section, Paul's (travel) plans, and the conclusion. The strengths of this commentary are its careful attention to linguistic details and its concern for the gospel.

Gager, John G. *Reinventing Paul.* Oxford: Oxford University Press, 2000.

Gager offers an accessible treatment of the new perspective on Paul. The new perspective asserts that Paul's negative statements about the Jewish Law were not intended toward Jews, but instead toward Gentiles. Paul speaks disparagingly about the Jewish Law in order to dissuade Gentiles from embracing it. Gager contends that Paul considered the Law still valid for Jews, even Jews who believed in Christ.

Gager also criticizes elements of the old perspective on Paul, including the notions that Paul converted to a wholly new religion and that Paul preached against the Jewish Law with its emphasis on works righteousness. Gager offers interpretive summaries of Galatians and Romans in the light of the new perspective.

Hays, Richard B. *Echoes of Scripture in the Letters of Paul.* New Haven: Yale University Press, 1989.

In the preface, Hays states the book's central question: How did Paul interpret Israel's scriptures? Hays maintains that the reader of Paul's Letters must question *how* to read Paul before asking *what* Paul says. Hays advances his agenda through a skillful combination of historical and literary approaches.

The book analyzes key features of Paul's reading of Jewish scripture, as well as the challenges that Paul's reading of Jewish scripture has created for subsequent generations. Furthermore, Hays emphasizes the centrality of the church in Paul's hermeneutics, which is an important departure from scholarship's usual focus on Paul's Christology (that is, beliefs about the nature and work of Jesus Christ).

Horsley, Richard A., ed. *Paul and Politics: Ekklesia, Israel, Imperium, Interpretation.* Harrisburg, Pa.: Trinity Press, 2000.

A unifying premise of this collection of essays is that Paul's Letters did and do have an effect on people's lives. The authors of these essays, who represent diverse social identities and who employ various methodologies, challenge the notion that Paul's Letters are purely spiritual texts to be appropriated by individual faith. Instead, the authors demonstrate how Paul's Letters addressed larger social and political issues such as Roman imperialism and slavery. Furthermore, the authors investigate the inherently political processes involved in interpreting biblical texts in general and Pauline texts in particular. This collection provides an excellent introduction to many of the debates in contemporary Pauline scholarship.

Käsemann, Ernst T. "The Saving Significance of the Death of Jesus in Paul." In *Perspectives on Paul*. London: SCM Press, 1971.

Käsemann examines Paul's emphasis on Jesus' crucifixion, contending that Paul's theology of the cross remains largely misunderstood in contemporary Christianity. The interpretation of Jesus' death as a sacrifice was not the dominant motif in Paul's theology. Instead, Paul added ideas of justification, reconciliation, and redemption to existing early Christian beliefs about the death of Jesus. Of equal importance to Paul was a theology of the word (that is, preaching about the Christ event). According to Käsemann, the theology of the cross and the theology of the word belong together.

_____. *Commentary on Romans*. Trans. Geoffrey W. Bromiley. Grand Rapids: William B. Eerdmans, 1980.

This commentary systematically examines the entire Letter of Romans, exploring the themes central to each division of the letter. Käsemann addresses topics such as: (1) the necessity for God to reveal God's righteousness to humanity; (2) the righteousness of God as the righteousness of faith; (3) the righteousness of faith as an actualization of eschatological freedom (that is, ultimate freedom from sin and death); (4) the righteousness of God and the problem of Israel; and (5) the righteousness of God in daily Christian life.

Keck, Leander E. *Paul and His Letters*. 2d edition. Philadelphia: Fortress Press, 1988.

According to Keck, there are often three main issues that engage academic and ecclesial interpreters of Paul: (1) the historical Paul; (2) the gospel of Paul; and (3) the assertions of Paul. Keck structures his work around these three categories. Also, he insists that Paul's identity is not synonymous with his letters. There is more to the conversation between Paul and his churches than modern interpreters, as an unintended audience, can hear.

The book examines the person of Paul in order to grasp who he was and the contexts from which he preached and wrote. Next, Paul's message is considered in order to grasp how one of the earliest Christian leaders viewed the Christ event, salvation, and the possibilities of proclamation. Finally, the book investigates the truth of Paul in order to grasp those realities that were most important to Paul, realities for which he fought.

Martyn, J. Louis. *Galatians*. New York: Doubleday, 1997.

In this commentary, Martyn attempts to hear Paul's Letter as the churches in Galatia heard it. He endeavors to keep one ear to the voice of Paul and one ear to the voices of the teachers—the Christian-Jewish evangelists who came to Galatia proclaiming a different message from Paul. This tension between voices forms the core of Martyn's commentary and informs his translation and understanding of the letter.

The interpretive details in this commentary are extraordinary. Moreover, the bibliography is impressive, as is Martyn's attention to the historical context of Galatians. Throughout the commentary, Martyn has placed a number of substantive yet accessible interpretive essays that further clarify elements discussed in the commentary.

Meeks, Wayne A. *The First Urban Christians: The Social World of the Apostle Paul*. New Haven: Yale University Press, 1983.

Examining the social dimensions of early Christianity as recorded in the Pauline Letters, this book attempts to describe common life patterns of Christians as they lived, worked, and worshiped. The book addresses topics such as: the first-century urban environment, the social status of Paul's congregants, civic models for the Pauline church, group cohesion, patterns of leadership and authority, and ritual and social experience. In this work, Meeks asserts that the reconstruction of *social* history is a central task of historical critical approaches to the New Testament.

Meyer, Paul W. "The Worm at the Core of the Apple: Exegetical Reflections on Romans 7." In *The Conversation Continues: Studies in Paul and John.* Robert T. Fortna and Beverly R. Gaventa, eds. Nashville: Abingdon Press, 1990.

This essay examines the problems that dogmatic theological concerns and anachronistic perspectives pose for historical-critical interpretations of Paul's Letters. Appealing to Romans 7 as an example, Meyer insists that theological dogma has often obscured Paul's argument in this portion of the letter. According to Meyer, interpretations of Romans 7 that have focused on whether Paul's statements refer either to pre-Christian or Christian experience miss that chapter's central and subtle claim.

Paul's purpose is not to denounce the Jewish law. Instead, he instructs his hearers on the pervasive power of sin to corrupt the best human piety, regardless of how that piety is expressed. Rather than being Paul's defense of Christianity over against Judaism, Romans 7 is an admission of the frailty of any religion when it is corrupted by sin.

Petersen, Norman R. *Rediscovering Paul: Philemon and the Sociology of Paul's Narrative World.* Philadelphia: Fortress Press, 1985.

Utilizing literary criticism and social anthropology, Petersen examines the centrality of narrative or story in Paul's thought. By story, Petersen means the process of imposing "a certain formal coherence on a virtual chaos of events." Through narrative devices such as point of view and plot, Paul's Letters present his perspectives on the world and on the various social possibilities he envisions.

More specifically, Petersen explores the story that emerges in Paul's Letter to Philemon. In this letter, hierarchies within a supposedly egalitarian church create an intricate network of social roles and relationships. According to Petersen, Paul utilizes this tension to exhort Philemon to accept Onesimus, the runaway slave, as a brother. Practically, such acceptance would include Philemon's manumission of Onesimus and the prohibition of any punitive action against Onesimus.

Sanders, E. P. *Paul and Palestinian Judaism: A Comparison of Patterns of Religion.* Philadelphia: Fortress Press, 1977.

Sanders investigates Paul's relationship to Judaism by analyzing the pattern of religion in Jewish customs and in Paul's Letters. According to Sanders, a pattern of religion consists of the means by which a believer enters and remains in a religion. The book is divided into two sections.

The first section explores Palestinian Judaism in light of diverse Jewish literature such as the Dead Sea Scrolls and the Apocrypha (that is, a group of books considered part of sacred scripture in Hellenistic Judaism and early Christianity). This section concludes with a historical treatment of the character of Palestinian Judaism. The second section addresses Paul's pattern of religion with respect to topics such as soteriology (that is, how people are saved from sin and destruction), the Jewish law, the human plight, covenantal nomism (namely, how people enter the saved community only through God's grace), works, and grace.

Segal, Alan F. *Paul the Convert: The Apostolate and Apostasy of Saul the Pharisee.* New Haven: Yale University Press, 1990.

As a Jewish scholar, Segal provides perspectives on Paul that many Christian interpreters often have not considered. According to Segal, Paul's radical, mystical conversion led to his career as a Christian apostle and Jewish apostate (that is, a defector from his previous religious commitments). Segal contends that Paul's religious experiences and visions situated him in the traditions of mystical and apocalyptic Judaism. Furthermore, he maintains that Paul's attempt to join together the Jewish and Gentile sectors of Christianity, as well as the demand for spiritual transformation of anyone joining the Christian sect, were consequences of Paul's personal experience as a convert to Christianity.

Stendahl, Krister. "The Apostle Paul and the Introspective Conscience of the West." In *Paul Among Jews and Gentiles and Other Essays*. Philadelphia: Fortress Press, 1976.

This essay attempts to clarify Paul's understanding of justification by faith. Stendahl maintains that the social relationship between Jews and Gentiles was a primary determinant in Paul's thought. Unlike his theological successors Augustine and Martin Luther, Paul did not struggle with a plagued conscience. Instead, Paul was concerned with the question of how to define the place for Gentiles in the church. According to Stendahl, the early church perceived correctly the issues with which Paul actually dealt. Those issues included: (1) What becomes of the law after the Messiah's coming? and (2) What impact does the Messiah's coming have on the relationship between Jew and Gentile? Also, Stendahl criticizes Western thinkers for imposing problems of conscience on Paul and his contemporaries. This imposition reflects modern dilemmas and does not accurately capture the central concerns of Paul.

Wire, Antoinette Clark. *The Corinthian Women Prophets: A Reconstruction Through Paul's Rhetoric*. Minneapolis: Fortress Press, 1990.

In an effort to uncover the voices of women in early Christianity, Wire provides a rhetorical analysis of 1 Corinthians. Her study focuses primarily on the views of the Christian women prophets in ancient Corinth. According to Wire, these women prophets had rejected male gender privilege, as well as the honor-shame system prevalent in Greco-Roman culture. Consequently, these women prophets encountered conflict with Paul who was still preoccupied with the assertion of status and authority so indicative of a patriarchal perspective.

LATE-BREAKING NEWS

s God's broadcasters, preachers report heavenly news. Heavenly news affects this world but comes from another world, where the sovereignty of God is already established. While giving to Caesar what belongs to Caesar, congregants come to the preaching moment hoping that God's reporter has some late-breaking news. "Preacher," they ask, "is there more to reality than what we are experiencing?"

Preachers should proclaim to their listeners that a relationship with God enables us to live in a different kind of world in the present even as we wait for a truly different world in God's future. The confident pronouncement that God has made available other options will inspire genuine Christian hope. Hope, according to the apostle Paul, is the realization that the best is yet to come (Rom. 8:18-25).

Furthermore, hope creates the calm assurance that there is some "news about God that circumstance cannot undermine or negate."[1] Global poverty, terrorism, and warfare have unleashed seismic shockwaves that have cracked, if not crumbled, many of our cultural structures and beliefs. Even as the ground shifts beneath our feet, preachers must report that God is the sure foundation that will outlast any catastrophe (1 Cor. 3:10-15).

Most news agencies pride themselves on providing late-breaking news. Whereas the news the preacher reports is more than two thousand years old, this news is as current as anything coming across the Associated Press's wire. Even now, some late-breaking news is coming across the wire from Rome . . .

The Roman military has just arrested a preacher named Paul for promoting treasonous behavior among Caesar's loyal subjects. Given the emperor's diminishing patience with these revolutionary followers of Jesus, Paul will likely meet an untimely death on Caesar's chopping block. The imperial authorities have asked Paul to recant his treasonous declarations.

Yet, in an amazing feat of courage—or fanaticism—Paul repeatedly declares: "For I am not ashamed of the gospel; it is the power of God for salvation to everyone who has faith, to the Jew first and also to the Greek."

Paul must really believe in this gospel, because it appears that he is going to die for it!

We now return you to your previously scheduled program.

NOTES

Introduction

1. Patrick J. Wilson and Beverly Roberts Gaventa contend, "Too many descriptions of the preaching task overlook [the] liturgical setting and functionally detach the sermon from worship." "Preaching as the Re-Reading of Scripture," *Interpretation* 52 (October 1998): 396.

2. See Paul Scott Wilson, *The Practice of Preaching* (Nashville: Abingdon Press, 1995), 20-36.

3. See Thomas W. Ogletree, "Dimensions of Practical Theology: Meaning, Action, Self," in *Practical Theology*, ed. Don S. Browning (San Francisco: Harper & Row, 1983), 83-101.

4. For evidence that reflection is itself a bodily doing and not simply an abstract affair of the mind, watch persons who are deep in thought. Inevitably, they will tap their fingers on a desk, rub their foreheads, pace the floor, or mark on a notepad.

5. Typically, some congregations expect a pastor to be a sophisticated Bible scholar, a learned theologian, a compassionate counselor, a polished public speaker, a fearless social prophet, an astute institutional administrator, and an effective fund-raiser.

6. So much has been written on the apostle Paul that scholars produce books *on the books* written about Paul. See the recent, useful annotated bibliography on Pauline scholarship by Mark A. Seifrid and Randall K. J. Tan, *The Pauline Writings: An Annotated Bibliography* (Grand Rapids: Baker, 2002).

7. *Ekklēsia*, which is the New Testament word for *church*, comes from the Greek verb "to call together" (*kaleō*). In ancient Greek culture, the *ekklēsia* was a decision-making body in a city. Thus, Paul employs a common concept among Greek speakers to describe the new communal arrangement created by Christ.

8. "Common era," which is often abbreviated C.E. is equivalent to the abbreviation A.D.

9. By "ideological" I mean the complex ways that persons merge beliefs and practices to exercise power with and over other groups of people.

10. Unless otherwise indicated, Torah refers to the full corpus of the Jewish Bible, including the Pentateuch, the Prophets, and the Writings, such as Psalms and Proverbs.

11. Having struggled sometimes to survive chaotic church business meetings, I can only imagine how challenging it must have been for Paul to build communities of Christ from scratch. Though I often take issue with certain things Paul wrote, I nevertheless applaud his courage in perilous circumstances. Generally speaking, if most American pastors "take a stand" for Christ, they might irritate some people, lose certain parishioners to other congregations, or (at worst) lose their jobs. In Paul's pastoral ministry, the costs of taking a stand for Christ were considerably more taxing and even lethal. Thus, when reading Paul's Letters, I strive not only to be *critical* (in the sense of discerning their contemporary meanings) but also *compassionate*.

12. Leander E. Keck, "The Accountable Self," in *Theology and Ethics in Paul and His Interpreters*, ed. Eugene H. Lovering Jr. and Jerry L. Sumney (Nashville: Abingdon Press, 1996), 1.

13. Donald H. Juel, "Multicultural Worship: A Pauline Perspective," in *Making Room at the Table: An Invitation to Multicultural Worship*, Brian K. Blount and Leonora Tubbs Tisdale, eds. (Louisville: Westminster John Knox Press, 2001), 44.

14. Later I will discuss the distinction between "authentic" and "inauthentic" Pauline Letters.

15. My colleague Samuel F. Weber, O.S.B. reminded me that the word *spiritual* is derived from the Latin word *spiritus*, which means "breath" or "wind." Thus, spirituality concerns those beliefs and practices dealing with the origin and destination of life's "breath." Spirituality raises foundational questions such as: From where does "breath" come? Where will our "breath" take us? And therefore, what is the ultimate meaning of life?

16. The Greek word for spirit is *pneuma*. Paul's uses of this word to refer to the Holy Spirit are numerous. For example, note his focus on the Spirit in Romans 8, 1 Corinthians 2, and Galatians 3.

17. Gordon D. Fee, *Paul, the Spirit and the People of God* (Peabody, Mass.: Hendrickson Publishers, 1996), 30.

18. Frederick C. Tiffany and Sharon H. Ringe, *Biblical Interpretation: A Roadmap* (Nashville: Abingdon Press, 1996), 61.

19. Richard Lischer, "Before Technique: Preaching and Personal Formation," *Dialog* 29 (1990): 182.

20. For representative attempts to "correct" the influence of Martin Luther on Pauline interpretation, see Krister Stendahl, *Paul Among Jews and Gentiles* (Philadelphia: Fortress Press, 1976); E. P. Sanders, *Paul and Palestinian Judaism* (Philadelphia: Fortress Press, 1977); Francis Watson, *Paul, Judaism and the Gentiles: A Sociological Approach* (Cambridge: Cambridge University Press, 1986); Elsa Tamez, *The Amnesty of Grace: Justification by Faith from a Latin American Perspective*, trans. Sharon H. Ringe (Nashville: Abingdon Press, 1993); and John G. Gager, *Reinventing Paul* (New York: Oxford University Press, 2000).

21. See, for example, Romans 1:14-17; 1 Corinthians 1:23-31, 9:19-23; 2 Corinthians 8–9 (where Paul urges Gentile Christians to provide funds for impoverished Jewish Christians in Jerusalem); and Galatians 3:26-29. "Race relations" between Jews and Gentiles are a major issue in Galatians. For further discussion, see Brad Ronnell Braxton, *No Longer Slaves: Galatians and African American Experience* (Collegeville, Minn.: Liturgical Press, 2002).

22. In light of the rapid growth of Christianity among people of color in Africa, Latin America, and Asia, it might be inaccurate to refer any longer to white North American Christian congregations as "mainline." Philip Jenkins writes, "By 2025, 50 percent of the Christian population will be in Africa and Latin America, and another 17 percent will be in Asia." "The Next Christianity," *Atlantic Monthly* (October 2002): 55 and 58.

23. Brian K. Blount, *Then the Whisper Put on Flesh: New Testament Ethics in an African American Context* (Nashville: Abingdon Press, 2001), 126 (emphasis in the original).

24. James W. Thompson, *Preaching Like Paul: Homiletical Wisdom for Today* (Louisville: Westminster John Knox Press, 2001), 53-60.

25. For further discussion, see Raymond E. Brown, *An Introduction to the New Testament* (New York: Doubleday, 1997), 585-680.

26. Even though Paul might not have written these texts, they are obviously still part of the Christian Bible. Labeling them as "deutero-Pauline" does not eliminate the larger interpretive issue of the authority of the Bible in general and of texts promoting oppression in particular. I simply raise the possibility, indeed probability, that some of the blame has been wrongly cast upon Paul.

27. For a fuller treatment of this issue, see Brad Ronnell Braxton, *The Tyranny of Resolution: I Corinthians 7:17-24* (Atlanta: Society of Biblical Literature, 2000); Allen Dwight Callahan, Richard A. Horsley, and Abraham Smith, eds., "Slavery in Text and Interpretation," in *Semeia*

83/84 (1998); and C. Michelle Venable-Ridley, "Paul and the African American Community," in *Embracing the Spirit: Womanist Perspectives on Hope, Salvation and Transformation*, ed. Emilie M. Townes (Maryknoll, N.Y.: Orbis, 1997), 212-33.

28. In an excellent study, Wendy Cotter discusses these six women leaders: Apphia (Philem. 2); Chloe (1 Cor. 1:11); Prisca (1 Cor. 16:19, Rom. 16:3-4); Euodia and Syntyche (Phil. 4:2); and Phoebe (Rom. 16:1-2). "Women's Authority Roles in Paul's Churches: Countercultural or Conventional?" *Novum Testamentum* 36 (1994): 350-72.

29. Chloe might have been a patron to Paul and the Corinthian congregation, supplying some of their financial needs. Ibid., 368. Also, Acts 16:11-40 mentions Lydia's financial patronage to Paul.

30. In Romans 1, Paul emphasizes sexual *practices*. The contemporary concept of "sexual orientation" or "sexual identity" would have been foreign to Paul.

31. The scholarly literature concerning homosexuality and the Bible is immense. Some representative treatments include: Dale B. Martin, "Heterosexism and the Interpretation of Romans 1:18-32," *Biblical Interpretation* 3 (1995): 332-55; Robert Brawley, ed., *Biblical Ethics and Homosexuality: Listening to Scripture* (Louisville: Westminster John Knox, 1996); Robert E. Goss and Mona West, eds., *Take Back the Word: A Queer Reading of the Bible* (Cleveland: Pilgrim Press, 2000); and Robert A. J. Gagnon, *The Bible and Homosexual Practice: Texts and Hermeneutics* (Nashville: Abingdon Press, 2001).

1. What Is Preaching?

1. In spite of certain socially oppressive tendencies in the inauthentic Pauline Letters, these letters still provide rich theological and homiletical insights.

2. Olin P. Moyd, *The Sacred Art: Preaching and Theology in the African American Tradition* (Valley Forge, Pa.: Judson Press, 1995), 55.

3. Tom Beaudoin, *Virtual Faith: The Irreverent Spiritual Quest of Generation X* (San Francisco: Jossey-Bass, 1998), 87.

4. See Alister E. McGrath, "Theology of the Cross," in *Dictionary of Paul and His Letters*, Gerald F. Hawthorne, Ralph P. Martin, and Daniel G. Reid, eds. (Downers Grove, Ill.: InterVarsity Press, 1993), 192-97.

5. Womanist thinkers are black women who speak from and about the specific opportunities and challenges of being black women.

6. JoAnne Marie Terrell, *Power in the Blood? The Cross in the African American Experience* (Maryknoll, N.Y.: Orbis, 1998), 22.

7. Ibid., 33-34.

8. See Delores S. Williams, *Sisters in the Wilderness: The Challenge of Womanist God-Talk* (Maryknoll, N.Y.: Orbis, 1993), especially pp. 60-83 and 161-67.

9. Jacquelyn Grant contends that for many black women (and other oppressed persons) the *call to servanthood* has really meant a *compulsion to servitude*. "The Sin of Servanthood," in *A Troubling in My Soul: Womanist Perspectives on Evil and Suffering*, ed. Emilie M. Townes (Maryknoll, N.Y.: Orbis, 1993), 199-218.

10. Julie M. Hopkins, *Towards a Feminist Christology: Jesus of Nazareth, European Women, and the Christological Crisis* (Grand Rapids: William B. Eerdmans, 1994), 51-52.

11. Ibid., 50.

12. See Thomas Troeger's discussion of a distorted theology of the cross in *Preaching While the Church Is Under Reconstruction: The Visionary Role of Preachers in a Fragmented World* (Nashville: Abingdon Press, 1999), 58-63.

13. Tyron L. Inbody, *The Many Faces of Christology* (Nashville: Abingdon Press, 2002), 162.

14. For a fascinating interpretation of this parable, see Mary Ann Tolbert, *Sowing the Gospel: Mark's World in Literary-Historical Perspective* (Minneapolis: Fortress Press, 1989), 148-64.

15. Nils Alstrup Dahl, "The Crucified Messiah," in *Jesus the Christ: The Historical Origins of Christological Doctrine*, ed. Donald H. Juel (Minneapolis: Fortress Press, 1991), 32, 43.

16. Jürgen Moltmann, *The Crucified God* (Minneapolis: Fortress Press, 1993), 327.

17. Martin Luther King Jr., "Our Struggle," in *A Testament of Hope: The Essential Writings and Speeches of Martin Luther King, Jr.*, ed. James M. Washington (San Francisco: HarperSanFrancisco, 1986), 76.

18. Fred B. Craddock, "Is There Still Room for Rhetoric?" in *Preaching on the Brink: The Future of Homiletics*, ed. Martha J. Simmons (Nashville: Abingdon Press, 1996), 72.

19. Jeffrey D. Arthurs, "The Place of Pathos in Preaching," *The Journal of the Evangelical Homiletics Society* 1 (December 2001): 19.

20. James W. Thompson has a helpful discussion of Paul's pastoral preaching to the Thessalonians in *Preaching Like Paul: Homiletical Wisdom for Today* (Louisville: Westminster John Knox Press, 2001), 49-60.

21. Thomas G. Long, *The Witness of Preaching* (Louisville: Westminster John Knox Press, 1989), 34.

22. Thomas Edward Frank, *The Soul of the Congregation: An Invitation to Congregational Reflection* (Nashville: Abingdon Press, 2000), 35.

23. Paul Scott Wilson, *The Practice of Preaching* (Nashville: Abingdon Press, 1995), 31.

24. J. Ellsworth Kalas, *Preaching from the Soul: Insistent Observations on the Sacred Art* (Nashville: Abingdon Press, 2003), 30-34.

25. Warren H. Stewart Sr., *Interpreting God's Word in Black Preaching* (Valley Forge, Pa.: Judson Press, 1984), 57 (emphasis in the original).

26. Charles L. Bartow, *God's Human Speech: A Practical Theology of Proclamation* (Grand Rapids: William B. Eerdmans, 1997), 73.

27. Geffrey B. Kelly and F. Burton Nelson, eds., *A Testament to Freedom: The Essential Writings of Dietrich Bonhoeffer*, rev. ed. (San Francisco: HarperSanFrancisco, 1995), 86. Quoted in Troeger, *Preaching While the Church Is Under Reconstruction*, 79.

2. Who Was Paul?

1. Ben Witherington III, *The Paul Quest: The Renewed Search for the Jew of Tarsus* (Downers Grove, Ill.: InterVarsity Press, 1998), 297.

2. Ibid., 307.

3. The Pharisees were an influential Jewish group in the first century of the common era. They advocated for the reform of Judaism through rigorous Torah observance.

4. Daniel Boyarin, *A Radical Jew: Paul and the Politics of Identity* (Berkeley: University of California Press, 1994), 2.

5. Lawrence H. Schiffmann, *From Text to Tradition: A History of Second Temple Rabbinic Judaism* (Hoboken, N.J.: KTAV Publishing House, 1991), 105-6.

6. N. T. Wright, *What Saint Paul Really Said: Was Paul of Tarsus the Real Founder of Christianity?* (Grand Rapids: William B. Eerdmans, 1997), 26-29.

7. Helmut Koester, "Imperial Ideology and Paul's Eschatology in 1 Thessalonians," in *Paul and Empire: Religion and Power in Roman*

Imperial Society, ed. Richard A. Horsley (Harrisburg, Pa.: Trinity Press, 1997), 162.

8. Ibid.

9. Bruce W. Longenecker, "Narrative Interest in the Study of Paul," in *Narrative Dynamics in Paul: A Critical Assessment*, ed. Bruce W. Longenecker (Louisville: Westminster John Knox Press, 2002), 4.

10. In Romans 9:5, Paul comes close to referring to Christ as "God." Even there, ambiguity abounds. Depending on how one translates the verse, Paul might be referring to Jesus Christ as God, or his statement might apply to the God of Israel. Also, in the Christ hymn in Philippians 2, Paul cautiously says that Jesus Christ was "in the form of God."

11. For an intriguing discussion, see Charles H. Cosgrove, *Elusive Israel: The Puzzle of Election in Romans* (Louisville: Westminster John Knox Press, 1997).

12. John Koenig, "The Knowing of Glory and Its Consequences: 2 Corinthians 3–5," in *The Conversation Continues: Studies in Paul and John*, Robert T. Fortna and Beverly R. Gaventa, eds. (Nashville: Abingdon Press, 1990), 162.

13. Richard B. Hays, *The Moral Vision of the New Testament* (San Francisco: HarperSanFrancisco, 1996), 25.

14. Gordon D. Fee, *God's Empowering Presence: The Holy Spirit in the Letters of Paul* (Peabody, Mass.: Hendrickson Publishers, 1994).

15. Brendan Byrne observes, "'Flesh' and 'Spirit' do not denote separate elements in the make-up of human individuals ('body' and 'soul' for example) but rather two possibilities of human existence—the one self-enclosed, self-regarding and hostile to God, the other open to God and to life." *Romans* (Collegeville, Minn.: Liturgical Press, 1996), 238.

16. Luke Timothy Johnson, *Religious Experience in Earliest Christianity* (Minneapolis: Fortress Press, 1998), 8-9.

17. See John G. Gager, *Reinventing Paul* (New York: Oxford University Press, 2000), 43-75.

18. Richard Alston, *Aspects of Roman History, AD 14-117* (London: Routledge, 1998), 11-12.

19. Ibid., 15.

20. The imperial title "Caesar" comes from the name of Gaius Julius Caesar, the assassinated Roman leader. Augustus assumed the name Caesar from his great-uncle and father by adoption. Succeeding emperors employed the title.

21. James Rives, "Religion in the Roman Empire," in *Experiencing Rome: Culture, Identity and Power in the Roman Empire*, ed. Janet Huskinson (London: Routledge, 2000), 266.

22. Wayne A. Meeks, *The First Urban Christians: The Social World of the Apostle Paul* (New Haven: Yale University Press, 1983), 11.

23. Ibid., 17.

24. Robert Banks, *Paul's Idea of Community*, rev. ed. (Peabody, Mass.: Hendrickson Publishers, 1994), 26-27.

25. Richard A. Horsley, "1 Corinthians: A Case Study of Paul's Assembly as an Alternative Society," in *Paul and Empire: Religion and Power in Roman Imperial Society*, ed. Richard A. Horsley (Harrisburg, Pa.: Trinity Press, 1997), 242-52.

26. Antoinette Clark Wire, "The Politics of the Assembly in Corinth," in *Paul and Politics: Ekklesia, Israel, Imperium, Interpretation*, ed. Richard A. Horsley (Harrisburg, Pa.: Trinity Press, 2000), 125.

27. See the survey in Anthony Thacker, "Was Paul a Sexist?" *Epworth Review* 23 (1996): 85-94.

28. Judith M. Gundry-Volf, "Paul on Women and Gender: A Comparison with Early Jewish Views," in *The Road from Damascus: The Impact of Paul's Conversion on His Life, Thought, and Ministry*, ed. Richard N. Longenecker (Grand Rapids: William B. Eerdmans, 1997), 185.

29. See, for example, Antoinette Clark Wire, *The Corinthian Women Prophets: A Reconstruction through Paul's Rhetoric* (Minneapolis: Fortress Press, 1990), 45-47 and Elizabeth A. Castelli, *Imitating Paul: A Discourse of Power* (Louisville: Westminster John Knox Press, 1991).

30. David J. Williams, *Paul's Metaphors: Their Context and Character* (Peabody, Mass.: Hendrickson Publishers, 1999), 60.

31. Paul's harsh language in 1 Corinthians 4:18-21, though not commendable, might also be an attempt to assert his parental responsibility for "disciplining the family."

32. S. Scott Bartchy, "Undermining Ancient Patriarchy: The Apostle Paul's Vision of a Society of Siblings," *Biblical Theology Bulletin* 29 (Summer 1999): 77.

33. For a summary of some interpretations, see Craig S. Keener, *Paul, Women and Wives: Marriage and Women's Ministry in the Letters of Paul* (Peabody, Mass.: Hendrickson Publishers, 1992), 20-22.

34. Wire, *The Corinthian Women Prophets*, 118, 130.

35. Judith M. Gundry-Volf, "Gender and Creation in 1 Corinthians 11:2-16: A Study in Paul's Theological Method," in *Evangelium*

Schriftauslegung Kirche: Festschrift für Peter Stuhlmacher zum 65. Geburstag, Jostein Adna, Scott J. Hafemann, and Otfried Hofius, eds. (Göttingen, Germany: Vandenhoeck & Ruprecht, 1997), 162.

36. Ibid., 152-60. The relevant Greek words can be translated as "shame" or, in the case of the New Revised Standard Version, as "disgrace."

37. For a succinct review of interpolations theories, see L. Ann Jervis, "1 Corinthians 14:34-35: A Reconsideration of Paul's Limitation of the Free Speech of Some Corinthian Women," *Journal for the Study of the New Testament* 58 (1995): 51-59.

38. Wire, *The Corinthian Women Prophets*, 155.

39. Jervis, "1 Corinthians 14:34-35," 68.

40. Some scholars have debated the meaning of the Greek phrase translated "prominent among the apostles" (*episēmoi en tois apostolois*). They argue that the phrase should be translated, "well known to the apostles." This alternative translation would indicate that Andronicus and Junia were not themselves apostles. This debate is as much about our contemporary ideologies as it is about the ancient evidence. Some interpreters find it difficult to believe that Paul could consider a woman to be not only a minister, but also an apostolic colleague. For further discussion, see Byrne, *Romans*, 453.

41. Morna D. Hooker, "The Letter to the Philippians," *The New Interpreter's Bible*, vol. 11 (Nashville: Abingdon Press, 2000), 540.

3. Paul as a Messenger of the Gospel

1. Daniel Patte, *Preaching Paul* (Philadelphia: Fortress Press, 1984), 17.

2. The *lectio divina* understanding of scripture began in the New Testament period and was developed by early church interpreters such as Origen, Saint Augustine, and Saint Benedict. *Lectio divina* assumes that readers have had previous engagements with scripture in the worship and preaching of the church. Under the direction of the Holy Spirit these previous engagements with scripture penetrate believers' hearts, compelling them to ask: What must we do in response to scripture? The aim of *lectio divina* is to inspire greater devotion to God and to spiritual transformation. Hence, I refer to this approach to scripture as "devotional."

3. Mariano Magrassi, *Praying the Bible: An Introduction to Lectio Divina*, trans. Edward Hagman (Collegeville, Minn.: Liturgical Press, 1998), 72.

4. Eunjoo Mary Kim, *Preaching the Presence of God: A Homiletic from an Asian American Perspective* (Valley Forge, Pa.: Judson Press, 1999), 97.

5. Michael Casey, *Sacred Reading: The Ancient Art of Lectio Divina* (Liguori, Mo.: Liguori/Triumph, 1996), 11.

6. In devotional interpretation, both the reading of and meditating on scripture are vocal experiences. A person reads aloud the scripture so that the truth takes hold of a person's heart. This is the meaning of Psalm 37:30: "The mouths of the righteous utter wisdom." This utterance connotes a repeated murmuring of scripture in an almost musical fashion. This musical repetition of the scripture inspires a person to fall more deeply in love with the truth. Examples of this repetitive, vocal, and musical approach to scripture are found in various Catholic, Lutheran, and African American worship traditions.

7. For Paul baptism is a symbolic gesture demonstrating a person's allegiance to Christ and willingness to identify with Christ's suffering and death. In baptism, believers bury their former lives that were dominated by sin. Baptism also has significant communal dimensions. Baptism into Christ establishes a relationship of belonging. Believers belong to Christ and to the community of Christ. Consequently, believers must be mindful of their behaviors toward one another. See Richard P. Carlson, "The Role of Baptism in Paul's Thought," *Interpretation* 47 (1993): 255-66.

8. Charles E. Hummel, *Tyranny of the Urgent*, revised and expanded edition (Downers Grove, Ill.: InterVarsity Press, 1994).

9. James Forbes, *The Holy Spirit and Preaching* (Nashville: Abingdon Press, 1989), 21-23.

10. Gregg Braden, *The Isaiah Effect: Decoding the Lost Science of Prayer and Prophecy* (New York: Three Rivers Press, 2000), 96-98.

11. Luke Johnson rightly insists that in Acts 2 when the Holy Spirit is poured upon the church the real miracle takes place in the people's hearing, not in the speaking in tongues. *Religious Experience in Earliest Christianity* (Minneapolis: Fortress Press, 1998), 111.

12. C. S. Lewis, *The Screwtape Letters* (New York: Simon & Schuster, 1961), 20-21.

4. Interpreting Paul's Letters for Proclamation

1. Victor Paul Furnish, *The Moral Teaching of Paul: Selected Issues*, 2d and revised edition (Nashville: Abingdon Press, 1985), 17-18.

2. For more comprehensive discussions, see Frederick C. Tiffany and Sharon H. Ringe, *Biblical Interpretation: A Roadmap* (Nashville: Abingdon Press, 1996); Sandra M. Schneiders, *The Revelatory Text: Interpreting the New Testament as Sacred Scripture*, 2d ed. (Collegeville, Minn.: Liturgical Press, 1999); and Michael J. Gorman, *Elements of Biblical Exegesis: A Basic Guide for Students and Ministers* (Peabody, Mass.: Hendrickson Publishers, 2001).

3. Katie Geneva Cannon, *Teaching Preaching: Isaac Rufus Clark and Black Sacred Rhetoric* (New York: Continuum, 2002), 50 (emphasis mine).

4. Gerald L. Bruns, "Midrash and Allegory: The Beginnings of Scriptural Interpretation," in *The Literary Guide to the Bible*, Robert Alter and Frank Kermode, eds. (Cambridge, Mass.: Harvard University Press, 1987), 627.

5. Ibid., 628.

6. Nancy Lammers Gross, *If You Cannot Preach Like Paul ...* (Grand Rapids: William B. Eerdmans, 2002), 17.

7. Richard B. Hays, *Echoes of Scripture in the Letters of Paul* (New Haven: Yale University Press, 1989), 55.

8. Tiffany and Ringe, *Biblical Interpretation: A Roadmap*, 68.

9. Nancy Gross rightly emphasizes that sermon creation is not an afterthought in the interpretive process. Sermon creation commences at the very moment textual interpretation begins. See Gross, *If You Cannot Preach Like Paul ...*, 71-105.

10. Richard F. Ward, *Speaking of the Holy: The Art of Communication in Preaching* (St. Louis: Chalice Press, 2001), 58.

11. See Youtha C. Hardman-Cromwell, "Imaging the Sermon," *The African American Pulpit* (Winter 2002–2003): 18-20.

12. Robert Cummings Neville, *The God Who Beckons: Theology in the Form of Sermons* (Nashville: Abingdon Press, 1999), 9.

13. See the thorough and helpful list of theological questions in Paul Scott Wilson, *God Sense: Reading the Bible for Preaching* (Nashville: Abingdon Press, 2001), 69-71.

14. Tiffany and Ringe, *Biblical Interpretation: A Roadmap*, 32.

15. Peter J. Gomes, *The Good Book: Reading the Bible with Mind and Heart* (New York: William Morrow, 1996).

16. Thomas G. Long, *The Witness of Preaching* (Louisville: Westminster John Knox), 86.

17. Henry H. Mitchell, *Celebration and Experience in Preaching* (Nashville: Abingdon Press, 1990), 52-53.

18. Ibid., 51.

5. Proclaiming the News from Paul's Letters

1. A paraphrase from Haddon W. Robinson, foreword to *Preaching that Connects: Using the Techniques of Journalists to Add Impact to Your Sermons*, Mark Galli and Craig Brian Larson (Grand Rapids: Zondervan, 1994), 10.

2. The late Sandy Ray was the renowned pastor of Cornerstone Baptist Church in Brooklyn, New York.

3. Homiletical scholarship now discusses the *performance* aspects of effective preaching in an open and approving manner. See, for example, Jana Childers, *Performing the Word: Preaching as Theatre* (Nashville: Abingdon Press, 1998) and Richard F. Ward, *Speaking of the Holy: The Art of Communication in Preaching* (St. Louis: Chalice Press, 2001). The African American churches that nurtured me encouraged and even demanded that preachers incorporate dramatic and stylistic features into their sermons.

4. These lyrics are from the hymn, "I Heard the Voice of Jesus Say," in *The New National Baptist Hymnal* (Nashville: National Baptist Publishing Board, 1977), 310.

5. Ralph West is the noted pastor of the Church Without Walls in Houston, Texas.

6. Lee Ramsey cautions preachers about always appearing as heroic caregivers in their sermons. See *Care-full Preaching: From Sermon to Caring Community* (St. Louis: Chalice Press, 2000), 84-88.

7. Paul Scott Wilson, *The Practice of Preaching* (Nashville: Abingdon Press, 1995), 51-52.

8. Edward Corbett and Robert Connors insist, "The euphony and rhythm of sentences undoubtedly play a part in the communicative and persuasive process—especially in producing emotional effects." *Classical Rhetoric for the Modern Student*, 4th ed. (New York: Oxford University Press, 1999), 363.

9. See the helpful discussion about sermon introductions in Galli and Larson, *Preaching that Connects*, 35-46.

10. The different capitalization of the words *Sin* and *sin* is intentional. Sin with a capital *S* connotes the cosmic force that opposes the will of God, and sin with a lower case *s* connotes individual moral transgressions resulting from human captivity to this malevolent cosmic force. In the actual proclamation of this sermon, I readily employ rhetorical techniques such as gestures and intonation in order to clarify the distinction between *Sin* and *sin*. For example, when I refer to *Sin*, I frequently draw in the air an imaginary capital *S* with my hands and use a louder, more resonant voice.

11. African American preaching traditions emphasize the necessity of poetic license and homiletical creativity. Consequently, when I have preached this sermon, I have actually inserted a roll call of local funeral homes that we should contact in order to handle the "funerals" occurring. Congregations (of different denominations and ethnicities) have responded favorably to this homiletical tactic. First, the roll call displays a degree of homiletical creativity. Second, it demonstrates my concern for and connection with the local details of the community.

12. Typically, this section of the sermon has been a time of great congregational participation and celebration. In African American congregations, parishioners often have become more vocally and even bodily involved with each repeated phrase of the "thank-you note." As parishioners hear the words of the "thank-you note," they have often stood to their feet, waved their hands, and begun to voice their own gratitude to God. Even when I preached this sermon in a white congregational context, I saw among the white parishioners signs of more intense involvement during this part of the sermon, including nods of affirmation and changed facial expressions.

Epilogue

1. Walter Bruggemann, *Cadences of Home: Preaching Among Exiles* (Louisville: Westminster John Knox Press, 1997), 3 (emphasis in the original).

INDEX